"In this book Patrick Nix talks about the greatest hero of all time. I thought I knew King David's story pretty well. Man, was I in for a surprise! I never realized how many lessons David learned from his father, Jesse. After reading this book, you and your son will look at life quite differently. Among other things, your son will have more confidence, courage, and faith to face the future. Why wait? The game clock is ticking. Start reading!"

—Pat Williams, best-selling author, speaker, and senior vice president of the NBA Orlando Magic

"What football fan would be happy if all he knew about a football season was this headline: 'Auburn Wins National Championship'? Indeed, fans want the whole story: How it happened, who made it possible, and why things turned out as they did. What about this headline: 'David Defeats Goliath'? Wouldn't it be great to know the back story behind that historic battle? College football coach Patrick Nix opens up all the gritty details of this classic Bible story — and he does so for one reason: To provide clear insight into father-son relationships. In *David Had a Dad*, Nix examines the many ways Jesse instructed and guided his son on his way to becoming the great king of Israel. Coach Nix provides the inside story of David and Jesse — while uncovering helpful insights into how to become a godly father."

—Dave Branon, award-winning sports writer and Discovery House editor

"As the president of a ministry that reaches out to well over a million young men every year, I see every day how the absence of a father is eroding countless American homes. Yet, even when dad is present, he can still be 'absent' in the sense of understanding how to mold his son. Using frequent sports analogies that dads can easily relate to, Coach Nix offers profound insights into how 21st century fathers can raise their sons to be world changers like the biblical King David. This is a must-read for all dads!"

—Les Steckel, veteran NFL coach and President/CEO of Fellowship of Christian Athletes

"Coach Nix has hit the nail on the head for dads. David, through the example of his dad Jesse, was inspired to become a warrior for the Lord. Their legacy now coaches us to live a life worthy of Jesus Christ standing up and cheering the life we have led for His glory."

—Dave Johnson, Olympic Bronze Medalist and Corban University's Director of Athletics

"No person is free to prosper until he receives the blessing of his father. David was far from a perfect man, but his blessing still was pivotal in the lives of his children. That's why he appears in the linage of our Lord. It is so great to see Coach Nix drive home the indispensable need for a father's blessing."

—Bill Glass, President/Founder, Bill Glass Champions For Today

"The single greatest contributing factor to many of the problems and illnesses that afflict this generation: the fading role of fathers in American life. I have been through six broken homes myself, have spoken in 10,000 public schools, and now head up Student Leadership University to train young champions. My verdict? Every man in America should read this book. It's written by a man's man — someone who understands the arena of big-time college sports and coaching today's young men. Simply put, if a Florida Gator recommends a book by an Auburn Tiger Quarterback, you know it must be inspiring!"

—Jay Strack, President and Founder, Student Leadership University, www.studentleadership.net

"When I read Patrick's book, *David Had a Dad,* it made me appreciate my father and my own role as a dad. The role of a father has been downplayed in society to the detriment of our children. I love how Patrick addresses critical issues of fatherhood in today's society. This book is like giving bread to the starved. Read this book!"

—Scott Dawson, Popular Conference Speaker, Evangelist, Author

"I believe sports mirrors the Christian life. In this book Patrick Nix succeeds in giving us a coach's perspective on one of the Bible's greatest stories. I know Patrick is passionate about preparing his players to win. So, get ready to be coached up on the fundamentals of faith, family, and finishing strong at home!"

—Roman Gabriel III, Radio Host, Evangelist, and President of Sold Out Ministries

"In *David Had a Dad*, Coach Patrick Nix reminds us that — without an engaged and believable dad — our sons may never be what they could be. As only a winning coach can, Nix draws our attention to the lives of David and Jesse and Jesus, illustrating the factors necessary in raising sons to become young men 'after God's own heart.' This is a must-read for every father who wants to make a difference in the life of his son."

—Rich Rollins, D.Min., coauthor of *Redeeming Relationships* and *Spiritual Fitness: A Guide to Biblical Maturity*

"Patrick Nix hits the nail on the head. Fathers want to do their fatherly role well. We just need someone to point us in the right direction and motivate us to do it. Nix coaches us and cheers us on with his missive from David's life. He enters into the fray with Goliath and gives us Jesse's perspective. It is a fresh way of seeing this great biblical episode from a father's eyes. It is fast-paced, thought-provoking, and highly motivational. Read it!"

—Bruce W. Fong, Ph.D., renowned conference speaker, educator, author, and pastor of Sunset Church in San Francisco

"Coach Nix calls a great audible here. He takes the powerful story of David and digs away at the subtle and significant story of his father's influence."

—Keith Potter, Founder, The Champion Project

"I wish I had had this tool in my parenting bag. Patrick Nix's study of David goes well beyond the cute little Sunday school story of a sweet little shepherd boy killing a mighty giant. He has thoroughly studied the familiar events and developed a solid book with a significant number of helps for fathers raising sons."

—Scott McCord, Men's Ministry Director, Spring Mountain Bible Church, Clackamas, Oregon

"Using the classic David and Goliath story, Patrick Nix has taken one of the most pressing issues of our time, fatherhood, and created a modern-day masterpiece. In a class of its own, here is a book full of life lessons that no father can afford to miss out on."

—Chris Spicer, UK Bible teacher and author of *No Perfect Fathers Here*

"We often rush to the image of the battle without considering the training and preparation David needed to encounter Goliath. Patrick Nix keenly identifies the life-lessons we fathers need to impart upon our children as they prepare for the battlefields and opportunities of living as Christ-followers."

—Lane Cohee, author of *Letters to Our Next Generation: Life Lessons from a Father to His Sons*

"I cannot visualize a greater investment of my life than to raise up others with a 'heart for God.' Patrick is right on in his challenge to raise up leaders."

—Johnny M. Hunt, former SBC President, Pastor FBC Woodstock, Georgia

David Had a Dad:

Courageously Raising a Young Man After God's Own Heart

Patrick Nix

For my wife, Krista, and my children Emma Grace, Bo, Caleb, and Sara.
Being a husband and a father are my greatest joys in life.

"The Church is looking for better methods;
God is looking for better men."
　—E. M. Bounds

The author would love to hear from you.
You can write to him at DavidHadaDad@hotmail.com.

Additional copies of this book are available for sale online at
www.CreateSpace.com
www.BooksaMillion.com
www.BarnesandNoble.com
www.Amazon.com

Contents

Chapter 1
David Had a Dad

Now David was the son of an Ephrathite named Jesse (1 Samuel 17:12).

The Tale of the Tape

If you have ever watched a boxing match, you have seen and heard the tale of the tape during the introductions before the match begins. Each boxer makes his way to the ring with all his entourage and stands in his corner. Once both are standing in their respective corners, someone comes into the center of the ring to announce the fighters, as if we don't already know.

We have all heard the announcer say, "In the blue corner standing six feet tall weighing two hundred and twenty-three pounds, wearing blue trunks with white trim, hailing from Birmingham, Alabama..." Then come all the nicknames and accomplishments that can possibly be said. Each fighter is introduced and the match is ready to begin.

In the beginning of 1 Samuel 17, we are given the tale of the tape and the fighters in the classic battle of David and Goliath. On one hill you have the armies of the Philistines and on the other hill are the Israelites. The announcer comes out and gives us the tale of the tape. He begins with the Philistines and the mighty warrior they have chosen. Can't you just hear the announcer?

"In the Philistines' corner, from Gath, standing nine feet tall, wearing a bronze helmet, a scale of armor weighing five hundred shekels, wearing bronze greaves on his legs, with a bronze javelin on his back and holding a spear with an iron point weighing six hundred shekels, the mighty champion Goliath."

Wow! The announcer may have had to stop and catch his breath.

This description is based totally on Goliath's physical appearance. How big he is and how big and mighty his armor and equipment are. His description is very intimidating. He looks exactly the way everyone in his day viewed a mighty warrior. The only thing mentioned that is not about his physical appearance is where he's from, so not very many details of his upbringing. Did he have a father in the house? If so, what did his dad teach him? What was his family like? None of these details are mentioned, only the details of his outward appearance and it is impressive.

After catching his breath and letting the crowd quiet down, the announcer steps up to introduce Goliath's opponent. "Now, in the Israelites' corner, from Bethlehem in Judah, the son of Jesse, the youngest of eight sons, the shepherd boy David." What a contrast in the description of the two players in this battle. The Bible is more concerned with where David is from, who David's father is and his family situation than his outward appearance. There is nothing special about his outward appearance, but I believe the Bible is letting us know that David had something else that set him apart. One chapter earlier, in 1 Samuel 16:7b, God reminds Samuel that "man looks at the outward appearance, but the LORD looks at the heart." This speaks volumes to dads.

As fathers, we have much more to do with our boy's success or failure than do outward things. We try to give our boys the best of everything on the outside – education, cars, friends, sports equipment, etc. – but what they really need is their dad. They need us to be there, to invest in them, to teach them, to discipline them. While Goliath had all the physical stuff he needed, David had the dad he needed.

Dads often feel like they have to provide the biggest and best. We work all the time so we can afford to live in the nicest homes, in the nicest areas. We work all the time to send our boys to the best schools and sign them up in the best leagues. We work all the time to provide our boys with the best cars and equipment. We work all the time so our boys will not have to work as hard as we have. When we are not working we are busy with our hobbies and friends, but at least we have provided all the possessions our boys need to be successful, right?

Are we going about fatherhood all wrong—even with some of the best intentions? Maybe we are trying to provide our boys with what we did not have. We are trying to give them more. Or perhaps we just don't know what else to do. The description of Goliath and David in 1 Samuel gives us clear direction. Goliath has been provided everything. He has been given the biggest and the best. He is driving the nice cars. He lives in the nicest neighborhood. From a worldly perspective he has it all. Read verses 4-7; it is very impressive what this "champion" possesses. But something seems to be missing; who is his dad?

"Now David was the son of an Ephrathite named Jesse." Not much is told of Jesse other than he was old and had eight sons. But what is not written speaks as much for him as what is written. We do not read about what he has given David or how lofty a position he has obtained at work. We do read that he was a father. If you read the description of Goliath and David, you read that the difference between the two is Goliath had all the possessions he needed to be great, while David had a dad.

It is no accident the way the Bible describes the two main fighters in this battle. Clearly the world would choose the one who has a great outward appearance and all the tools, but God shows us there is something much more important — that is something only a dad can give.

I believe it is by design that God gives the description of the two warriors the way He does and I believe that as dads we had better not miss this. In this great story, a lesson can be learned of what a father gave to his son to allow him to defeat the giant. We will see the characteristics a father has instilled into "a man after God's own heart."

The way people describe our son tells us a lot about what we are doing for his future. If they only talk about how smart he is or what a strong arm he has, is that really what is important? Are we providing all the material and worldly things he needs but not providing the most important thing — ourselves? Our boys need their dads more than anything.

We must be careful of falling into the trap of giving our sons everything but us. What they really need and want is us. Not a bigger bat, a nicer car, a bigger house, or a certain school. They need and want their dads.

"Whose Son Is That Young Man?"

As Saul watched David going out to meet the Philistine, he said to Abner, commander of the army, "Abner, whose son is that young man?"

Abner replied, "As surely as you live, O king, I don't know."

The king said, "Find out whose son this young man is."

As soon as David returned from killing the Philistine, Abner took him and brought him before Saul, with David still holding the Philistine's head.

"Whose son are you, young man?" Saul asked him.

David said, "I am the son of your servant Jesse of Bethlehem." (1 Samuel 17:55-58)

The "tale of the tape" in 1 Samuel 17:12 is reinforced later in the chapter in verses 55-58. I am sure Saul wanted to know what lineage this boy had come from, but I believe there is more to it than just that. Where do you think David had learned these character traits? Do you think he just happened to have them? No, I believe God included this part to let men know how important it is for us to instill these qualities into our sons.

God wanted to make it clear that this was someone's son, not just any boy. Jesse had obviously done a great job and Saul wants to know who had raised this boy up to be such a stellar young man. What a great challenge for fathers! Do people ask, "Whose son is that?" about our sons? It is a great challenge to raise up a David, a man after God's own heart. I believe David learned these qualities from his dad, just like our sons are learning qualities from us, as their fathers.

David is referred to as "the son of Jesse" numerous times in the Bible. Isaiah 11:1 says, "A shoot will come up from the stump of Jesse; from his roots a Branch will bear fruit." Why does it go back to Jesse and not Boaz or Obed? Or why not just say David? Acts 13:22 refers to David as the son of Jesse, not just "David." Romans 15:12 refers back to Isaiah 11:10, where once again it is "the Root of Jesse." First Samuel 16:1 tells us that God sent Samuel "to Jesse of Bethlehem. I have chosen one of his sons to be king." It seems to all go back to David's father, Jesse.

God has given us a role as earthly fathers. Yes, God is our ultimate father and He is the one who we as fathers should try to emulate. But God is not writing in code here. David is mentioned as the son of Jesse more than fifteen times in the Bible. One or two may not mean much, but when this much ink is given to the father of the one whom God calls a man after His own heart, I believe fathers need to pay attention.

Are there lessons we can learn from the way David was raised? Can we get a glimpse into the heart that is like our heavenly father's? I believe so. Like Jesse, I believe we can raise our boys to be men after God's own heart.

"Train Up a Child"

One way to see how someone was raised is to watch how they raise their own children. This seems to be true of David and can be seen in the examples Solomon gives us about his dad, David. In Proverbs 4:3, Solomon tells us his dad taught him when he was young. David did not wait until Solomon was old and had already learned from others. David laid the spiritual foundation himself.

I have to believe David learned this valuable lesson from his dad, Jesse. Based on what's recorded in Scripture, we know David was parented well. Traditionally, it was usually the father who would have played the biggest part in David's upbringing.

Although Scripture does not say to what extent Jesse shaped David, we can safely assume that — as his father — Jesse played a monumental part in impacting David's character. David was "only a boy" (1 Samuel 17:42) when he encountered Goliath. Although he was only a youth, he had learned and been taught many great lessons that would help him defeat the giant. If Jesse had decided to wait until David was older to instill values such as trust in God and boldness, it would have been too late.

Solomon reemphasizes this again in Proverbs 22:6 when he tells us to, "Train up a child in the way he should go, and when he is old he will not turn from it." Jesse had trained up David from a young age and although he made mistakes in his life, when David was older, he had a solid foundation to fall back on. From reading Proverbs and Ecclesiastes we learn that David trained up Solomon when he was young and although Solomon made mistakes later in his life, he did have a strong foundation.

How are we training up our boys? Are we even training them? It seems that today many of us are relying on Sunday school teachers, school teachers, coaches, and moms to train up our boys. We are too busy trying to provide the stuff they need. We are raising Goliaths instead of Davids and if we are not careful, it will be too late to lay a solid foundation. Our sons will be hit right in the forehead with a stone and the next thing we know their heads will be cut off. We have to get into the battle early with our boys.

Training boys when they are young ensures that when they are old, they will have a firm foundation to stand on.

The Difference a Dad Can Make

Bill Glass is a former NFL player who has had a prison ministry for years. He tells a story that illustrates the tremendous power a dad has on his son. One time after doing a presentation at a prison, Bill had a conversation with one of the inmates who was a former Major League Baseball catcher. Bill asked the former player, "How did you become such a great catcher?"

The answer was not something Bill expected from a professional athlete. Most people would expect the answer to be like a description of Goliath, all physical. Instead, it sounded more like one from David. The former catcher told Bill that from a very young age his dad had told him that he was going to be a Major League Baseball catcher one day and that he did not want to disappoint his father. This, however, is only part of the story.

Another inmate who was standing close by interrupted, "That's funny. That's the same reason I'm in prison." See, the second inmate's father had told him since an early age he would end up in prison one day.

What a difference the words of a dad make. We have such an impact on our sons. Not only do they not want to disappoint us, but they also believe what we teach and what we tell them about who they can be and what they can do. It is a father's job and responsibility to build a foundation in our sons that will enable them to be men after God's own heart.

We cannot be afraid to go deep with our sons. For most men this is not natural. We may not be the communicators our wives are. We are probably not around as much as our wives are. Yet we cannot rely on our wives, our kid's coaches, schools, or even churches to do our job as a dad. We must be willing to ask and answer the tough questions of our sons. Fathers need to be the ones to teach sons what it means to be godly. The deeper we go, the stronger they will become. We must be willing to build a deep foundation with our boys so they can grow tall.

I visited New York City a few summers ago and while I was there I went to the site of the World Trade Center. Well, obviously, there was nothing there except two great big holes because of the horrific events of 9/11. But the two holes spoke volumes to me. I have talked to my players before about building on a solid foundation and that the deeper you dig the foundation the higher you can build. Seeing the large, deep foundations on which these two buildings were built helped me understand what is necessary in order to have an impressively large building.

The Bible tells us in Luke 6:48 that a real follower of Jesus "is like a man building a house, who dug down deep and laid the foundation on rock." We can help our sons do the same thing. We have to dig a deep foundation if we expect them to go high. If we do not dig deep, our sons will not be able to grow tall. You know the old saying, "The sky is the limit." If a boy tries to reach the stars without a deep foundation he will do nothing but crumble and fall.

I believe Jesse dug deep with David and instilled some character traits that gave him a foundation to be one of the greatest world leaders of all time. We have the same opportunity to dig deep and teach our sons the same character traits.

How Do They Describe You?

When people describe us, what do they say? Do they describe us like Goliath is described? Maybe they talk about the great job we have. It could be the vacation home we own or the kind of car we drive. Or do they talk about all the committees we are on? Do they only talk about our earthly treasures? None of these things are bad unless we allow them to become who we are. If this is all we have, then we have nothing, and like Goliath, one day we too will die an eternal death.

I want to be described the way David was described. I want to be known as someone's son. Galatians 3:26 says, "You are all sons of God through faith in Jesus Christ." I want to be known as a son of God. I want people to know that I am an heir to the throne of the Almighty God, and no matter what happens I will praise Him. If this is how we are described, then like David one day we will have ultimate victory and have eternal life.

What's your tale of the tape?

Get in the Game!

Here is your opportunity to make this first chapter real in your own life...

David Had a Dad: *1 Samuel 17:1-13*

1 Now the Philistines gathered their forces for war and assembled at Sokoh in Judah. They pitched camp at Ephes Dammim, between Sokoh and Azekah. 2 Saul and the Israelites assembled and camped in the Valley of Elah and drew up their battle line to meet the Philistines. 3 The Philistines occupied one hill and the Israelites another, with the valley between them.

4 A champion named Goliath, who was from Gath, came out of the Philistine camp. His height was six cubits and a span. 5 He had a bronze helmet on his head and wore a coat of scale armor of bronze weighing five thousand shekels; 6 on his legs he wore bronze greaves, and a bronze javelin was slung on his back. 7 His spear shaft was like a weaver's rod, and its iron point weighed six hundred shekels. His shield bearer went ahead of him.

8 Goliath stood and shouted to the ranks of Israel, "Why do you come out and line up for battle? Am I not a Philistine, and are you not the servants of Saul? Choose a man and have him come down to me. 9 If he is able to fight and kill me, we will become your subjects; but if I overcome him and kill him, you will become our subjects and serve us." 10 Then the Philistine said, "This day I defy the armies of Israel! Give me a man and let us fight each other." 11 On hearing the Philistine's words, Saul and all the Israelites were dismayed and terrified.

12 Now David was the son of an Ephrathite named Jesse, who was from Bethlehem in Judah. Jesse had eight sons, and in Saul's time he was very old. 13 Jesse's three oldest sons had followed Saul to the war: The firstborn was Eliab; the second, Abinadab; and the third, Shammah.

The Snap:

Describe the scene.

Who are the players?

What is the difference between the two players?

The Pass:

"For the wages of sin is death, but the gift of God is eternal life in Christ Jesus our Lord." Romans 6:23

Describe the scene portrayed in this important New Testament verse.

Who are the players?

What are the differences between the players?

The Catch:

Read Mark 8:36, 1 John 1:9

Are you going to be a David or a Goliath?

Chapter 2
Know Your Role

Now David was the son of an Ephrathite named Jesse, who was from Bethlehem in Judah. Jesse had eight sons, and in Saul's time he was old and well advanced in years. Jesse's three oldest sons had followed Saul to the war: The firstborn was Eliab; the second, Abinadab; and the third, Shammah. David was the youngest. The three oldest followed Saul, but David went back and forth from Saul to tend his father's sheep at Bethlehem (1 Samuel 17:12-15).

DAVID'S HEART

David realized and accepted the role God gave him and did it to the best of his ability. While his three older brothers went with Saul to fight the war, David's role was to stay home and tend his father's sheep. This was definitely not a prestigious job, but it had to be done. Earlier, David had been in the company of King Saul and was even one of his armor-bearers (1 Samuel 16:21). David had already been anointed as the next king by Samuel (1 Samuel 16:13).

David knew who he was and what he was destined to do. However, David's current role was to go back home and tend the sheep. It may have been tough and even humiliating for David to have such a passive role but he was faithful where he was. In the same way, in our differing roles — husband, brother, son, employee, friend, or team member — when we faithfully accept where God has placed us, we can be used by Him in each role.

If David had gone to the war with his brothers on the first day, the story would have a different ending. Either David would have been with the crowd of

Israelites who ran and hid in fear, or he would have killed Goliath on the first day. I personally believe David would have killed Goliath on day one. This would have left little room for God to get the glory, and that is why we are here, to glorify God.

First Peter 5:6 tells us to "humble yourselves, therefore, under God's mighty hand, that He may lift you up in due time." If we will humble ourselves to take on the routine role of the shepherd, He will lift us up in His time. There are times when God gives us roles away from the action. He had the perfect time for David to go to the war, but in the beginning He needed him to tend the sheep.

Sometimes God gives us these roles to prepare us for what is to come. We do not know what that may be, but we have to understand that God has put us in this role for this time. Some roles are easier for me to embrace than others, but embrace them I must.

Even when circumstances feel unfair or even demeaning, embracing God's plan for us is a sign of maturity in Christ. Genesis 50:20 says, "You intended to harm me but God intended it for good, to accomplish what is now being done." This was said by Joseph — sold into slavery, falsely accused and left to live out the remainder of his days in a prison in a foreign country, far away from his family and past life. Joseph expressed these words of faith, faith that God put him in certain situations and circumstances for good.

Similarly, David was given the role of shepherd as a boy in order to prepare him for God's good plans to come.

"But David"

...but David went back and forth from Saul to tend his father's sheep at Bethlehem (verse 15).

We have all had some "but David" moments in our lives, those moments when life just doesn't seem fair. Why am I not getting to go to the war? Why do I have to tend the sheep? We can just fill our own names in the blanks. But (name) did not get the job or the raise. But (name) did not get the girl. But (name) wasn't born into the right family. If we are not careful, these "but Davids" can become convenient excuses to underachieve.

One of my "but David" moments came my first three years in college.

I went to Auburn University on a football scholarship as a quarterback and I just knew things were going to be great. I had never sat the bench in my life, "but Patrick" would sit the bench for three years. I knew I might have to sit a year or two, but did not expect it to be three. It was not a very fun time in my football life. I thought I was ready and did not understand why I was not playing. As with David, God decided, "but Patrick" will be the back-up. That was to be my role. No, I did not particularly enjoy it, but I did it the best I could. I became our team's biggest cheerleader. I prepared myself to play; I tried to be as good of a leader as a backup quarterback can be. I had no idea I was going through a "but Patrick" season, but I was.

During those first three years of college, God was humbling me so He could lift me up in His time. If I would have played early, He would not have received all the glory. The right time and place were coming, but not yet. These years were a time for Him to prepare me for what was to come. I was not ready and He knew it, even though I did not. What would come later would be a life-changing event and I needed to keep growing and preparing to be ready for it.

My third year at Auburn, and my third year on the bench, was an unbelievable year for us. We were going into the last game of the year against our arch rival, who happened to be pretty good too, with a perfect record of 10-0. It was one of the biggest games in Auburn's history. Only one game left between us and a perfect season.

I had played my role as back-up quarterback very well. I had cheered and supported the best I could and had seen very limited reps. Only God knew what was to come. In the third quarter we found ourselves trailing 14-5. On a third down play our starting quarterback went down with an injury. It was now 4th and 15 with the ball on the 35 yard line. We decided to go for it on fourth down with the back-up quarterback now in the game.

Well, I got the play and went running on the field to call it in the huddle. It was a very simple play in which our best wide receiver, Frank Sanders, would line up on the left side and run a go route. I had practiced this throw many times that week and I cannot even begin to tell you how many times in my life I had practiced this throw. It was the biggest pass of my life and I was ready.

I caught the snap, dropped back and lofted the ball toward the end zone. Frank went up, made a great catch and dove in for a touchdown. We went on to win the game 22-14 and finished the year undefeated. Only God could orchestrate a moment like that. The back-up quarterback comes in to throw a touchdown pass on his first play without even taking a warm-up throw. Looking back I am so glad I had my "but David" years.

JESUS' HEART

There is no doubt Jesus knew His power. Like David, Jesus had been in the presence of a king — the King. In Matthew 11:27, Jesus claims to be the Son of God. In Mark 14:62, Jesus claims to be the Son of Man. In Luke 24:25-27, Jesus explains that He is the Christ. In John 3:16-17, Jesus claims to be the Son of God and our savior. He knew He was powerful, however, He also knew His role in salvation. Philippians 2:6-11 gives the best example of Jesus understanding His role.

> *Who, being in very nature God,*
> *did not consider equality with God something to be grasped,*
> *but made himself nothing,*
> *taking the very nature of a servant,*
> *being made in human likeness.*
> *And being found in appearance as a man,*
> *he humbled himself*
> *and became obedient to death—*
> *even death on a cross!*
> *Therefore God exalted him to the highest place*
> *and gave him the name that is above every name,*
> *that at the name of Jesus every knee should bow,*
> *in heaven and on earth and under the earth,*
> *and every tongue confess that Jesus Christ is Lord,*
> *to the glory of God the Father.*

Like David, Jesus' role was to tend the sheep. Except the "sheep" Jesus would tend were the souls of mankind. In Matthew 2:6, Jesus is called the shepherd of the people of Israel. Jesus refers to Himself as the shepherd in Matthew 26:31. John 10:11-12 gives us the best example of Jesus being a shepherd and of knowing His role: "I am the good shepherd; I know my sheep and my sheep know me—just as the Father knows me and I know the Father—and I lay down my life for the sheep." Jesus, like David, knew and accepted this role, even with its challenges.

"But Jesus"

But Jesus made no reply, not even to a single charge — to the great amazement of the governor (Matthew 27:14).

It is hard to comprehend that Jesus, "being in very nature God," could have "but David" moments in life, too. Yet He did. After all, He was, "made in human likeness" and had His struggles and moments of disappointment just like you and me. This verse in Matthew comes at a moment when Jesus knows that His life is hanging in the balance. Pilate is questioning Jesus — it is His last chance to save Himself. Just defend yourself, Jesus. Say something to explain away why you are here. "But Jesus made no reply, not even to a single charge."

Here is the ultimate "but David" moment: "but Jesus made no reply..."! David had to stay and tend his father's sheep instead of going into battle alongside his brothers. Jesus had to stand and keep His mouth shut...knowing He was going to be crucified, knowing He was completely innocent. Jesus had agonized over this situation (Matthew 26:39). He knew the pain He would have to endure. It is hard to fathom the discipline it took to keep His mouth shut and know His role. Pilate could not understand why Jesus did not defend himself. Jesus' silence was met with "great amazement" by Pilate.

Jesus could have called down legions of angels to defend and save Him (Matthew 26:53), but He knew this was not the will of the Father. He knew His role was not to be saved but to save. "But David" moments in life are not easy, but they do accomplish great things if we allow God to work. I am so glad Jesus knew His role and accepted it; if not, we would have no hope.

"Consider it Pure Joy"

If we have a personal relationship with Jesus Christ, we do not have to fear our "but David" moments at all. Romans 8:28 tells us, "that in all things God works for the good of those who love him." We can have comfort in the fact that, just like David and Jesus, God has everything under control for us as well.

Instead of viewing our "but David" moments in a negative light, we should "consider it pure joy" (James 1:2) when we face our "but David" times. We can be thankful God has given us a chance to grow and "in due time" He will lift us up. We will see later how David took advantage of this time in order to prepare to face Goliath.

LESSONS FROM JESSE

I can imagine Jesse looking at David and saying, "I know you are going to be the next king, but right now you are my son and you are going to tend the sheep." What an example for us as fathers. It is our responsibility to be the head of our households and to make decisions our children may not like. It is not our job to make our children happy but to raise them well.

Jesse knew David was not ready to go to the war yet. He had no idea of the ramifications of his decision, but he knew what David's role was at the present time. Most of us as fathers are the opposite of Jesse. We want our sons to be ahead in everything. We want them to start school early, play with the older boys in sports, learn to read before they ever get to school, etc. We want our sons to be in the advanced program of life. We push them into everything.

Jesse shows a different approach. It is likely that he viewed David as competent to handle stressful situations. David had already been ordained as the next king (1 Samuel 16:12-13) — and that carried plenty of pressure. Jesse went the other way. He took a slower approach. He knew God would work things out in His timing. Jesse continued to train up David to be the man he would need to be.

As fathers, we cannot miss this. Strong men are not grown from boys who skip stages. It is important to make sure our boy understands his roles in life. He will have to pay his dues. We cannot give them everything or throw them into situations too quickly. Let him grow up and go through the process.

The bottom line is for us to take our egos out of the equation and to look at what is best for our sons. It is not about my kid being better than yours, but my kid being the best he can be in the situation he is in, big or small.

Our ultimate role is that of Christian and we must be sure we are training our boys to understand their roles in relationship to Jesus Christ.

"Jesus Grew"

The ultimate example of a father making sure his kid knew how to do his role and having him wait until it was time is God with Jesus. Consider this: Jesus is God in the flesh. He could have done whatever He wanted, however He wanted to do it. But the Father took thirty years to prepare Jesus before He started His earthly ministry.

Luke 2:52 is one of my favorite verses; it gives us a glimpse into how God prepared Jesus. "And Jesus grew in wisdom and stature, and in favor with God and with man." This verse is one of the only links we have between Jesus' birth and His ministry. Not much is written about this time of His life, but this verse speaks volumes.

Just think: if Jesus had to grow, how much more do we have to grow or help our boys to grow? God knew Jesus would have to be developed in all four areas before He would be ready for His ultimate calling.

Let's take a quick look at all four areas because I believe they are essential to anyone's development, and especially to our sons.

First, we see that Jesus grew in wisdom. Traditionally wisdom is seen as the ability to apply knowledge or experience or understanding or common sense and insight. The Bible tells us that the beginning of wisdom is the fear of the Lord. I believe even Jesus had to develop in these ways: He had to develop this awe and respect of His Father. He also had to gain earthly knowledge, experiences, develop common sense, and understand how to put these together. Remember, although Jesus was, and is, fully God, He is also fully human.

Proverbs 4:3-9 tells us as fathers that we must demand that our sons get wisdom and hold on to it. As fathers we must instill a fear of the Lord in our sons, and one sure way is for them to see this awe and respect in us. We must fear the Lord ourselves. We must also allow our boys to gain the knowledge, experiences, understanding, and insight they will need in life. And it takes time for them to attain this.

Second, we see that Jesus grew in stature. Obviously Jesus got older, and therefore grew in size. But there is more here than meets the eye. God put this in the Bible for a reason. I believe He knew how difficult the challenge Jesus faced was going to be. Jesus had to be strong physically and be ready to meet the demands His body would face. We have to let our sons develop in stature and grow in the right way, too.

In our society this is not as easy as it sounds. With a steady diet of fast food and quick on-the-go meals, we tend to be more concerned with hurrying up and getting them to their next event than we are with making sure they are healthy. We must follow God's example and take care of our kid's stature. Our boys are in for tough physical battles.

Third, Jesus grew in favor with God. Wow! This is absolutely incredible to me. Jesus — who is fully God and at the same time fully man — had to grow in favor with God. We must make sure that personally we are growing in favor with God and that our sons are growing in favor with God, too.

Although we do not see exactly how Jesus did this, we can see the fruit of it in His three years of ministry. We constantly read of Jesus consecrating time to prayer, meditating on Scripture, and ministering to others in ways that glorified God. These are the three essentials of growing closer to the Lord.

James 4:8 tells us that if we come near to God, He will come near to us. The more we seek Him through prayer, His word, and fellow believers, the more we will find Him.

Finally, Jesus grew in favor with man. Growing and learning to respect and work with those around us is essential. Jesus did not necessarily have to have help from humans, but that was the way God designed His plan. God chose for Jesus to grow in favor with man and to allow man to help Him. We must do the same with our sons. Jesus shows us the ultimate example of teamwork. God could have found another way, but that was not His plan. Jesus accepted His role in this plan and allowed humans to help Him save a lost world. Although Jesus' role was the most important, He still realized His need for others, and we should do the same.

Like God and Jesse, we must be sure our sons know their roles. We cannot let them go too fast and skip this process, as hard as it is. We as dads must be willing to help guide our boys through this process. We may actually have to spend some time going through the process of finding our own roles and growing in wisdom, stature, favor with God and man. Thankfully, it is never too late.

Get in the Game!

Here is your opportunity to make this second chapter real in your own life...

Know Your Role: *1 Samuel 17:12-15*

12 Now David was the son of an Ephrathite named Jesse, who was from Bethlehem in Judah. Jesse had eight sons, and in Saul's time he was old and well advanced in years. 13 Jesse's three oldest sons had followed Saul to the war: The firstborn was Eliab; the second, Abinadab; and the third, Shammah. 14 David was the youngest. The three oldest followed Saul, 15 but David went back and forth from Saul to tend his father's sheep at Bethlehem.

The Snap:

What were David's roles?

What do these verses say about David?

1 Samuel 16:1, 7-13 and 1 Samuel 16:21

The Pass:

Read *Philippians 2:6-11*

What does this say about the role Jesus played?

What do these verses say about Jesus?

Mark 14:61-62, John 3:16-17, Matthew 27:14

The Catch:

What roles do each of us have?

How does the Bible teach us to handle these roles?

1 Peter 5:6

How does the Bible teach us to handle our "but David" moments?

Romans 8:28, James 1:2-4

Chapter 3
Do Your Job

Now Jesse said to his son David, "Take this ephah of roasted grain and these ten loaves of bread for your brothers and hurry to their camp. Take along these ten cheeses to the commander of their unit. See how your brothers are and bring back some assurance from them. They are with Saul and all the men of Israel in the Valley of Elah, fighting against the Philistines." Early in the morning David left the flock with a shepherd, loaded up and set out, as Jesse had directed (1 Samuel 17:17-20).

DAVID'S HEART

If we had not heard the story of David and Goliath our whole lives, these verses would not seem very important. These verses are nothing more than a dad giving his son a routine job to do. David was basically given the job of errand boy or go-fer.

Jesse does not tell David, "Hey, this big bully named Goliath needs to be taken care of. Take off to the battle and kill him." No, it was nothing like that. David was simply instructed to take supplies to his brothers and their commander, see how they were doing, and bring back their tithes (see NIV footnote). There was no way David knew how this seemingly meaningless job would radically change his place in history.

In these verses, there are three jobs David performed. First, he was tending the sheep. Second, he found a replacement shepherd to care for the sheep during his absence. Third, he immediately responded to his father's instructions. Let's take a closer look at each of these.

As Working for the Lord

First of all, we read that David was doing the job he was initially given. We know David had been tending the sheep for at least forty days. First Samuel 17:16 tells us that Goliath had already come out and defiantly stood against the Israelites for forty days. David did the job he was given, and by all indications he was doing the job well (verses 34-35). He may or may not have understood the big picture, but he did understand his job was to tend the sheep.

In life, it seems like the meaningless jobs we often take for granted and do not do to the best of our ability. We get someone else to do them or we just do not do them at all. As we saw in the previous chapter, David had already been anointed the next king; tending sheep seemed to be a little beneath a future king. However, David understood his role and knew that tending the sheep was the job he had been given, and he was going to do it well.

How many times are we given what seem like meaningless jobs? These jobs are underappreciated and can be done by anyone. However, like David, it is the job we have been given so we should do it to the best of our ability.

Colossians 3:23 tells us that whatever we do, we should do it with all of our heart as though we were working for the Lord. Do we view every job as an assignment from God? No matter how big or small the job, we should do it with all our hearts.

We must understand that our jobs do not come from man but from God. God had a purpose for sending David to tend the sheep, and He has a purpose for every job He gives us.

Entrusted to You by God

Second, David made sure the sheep were taken care of before he left. There is no evidence that his father told him to make sure he had someone else watch the sheep, but any good shepherd knows that even though he may have to leave the sheep for a time, the sheep still need someone to watch them. I am sure David was very excited to get to the battle, but not so excited that he neglected his duties.

The sheep had been entrusted to David, and it was his job to take care of them. We too have been entrusted with many things. In 1 Timothy 6:20, Paul urges Timothy to, "guard that which has been entrusted to you." I believe God urges us to do the same with what He has entrusted to us. As a husband, God has entrusted us with a wife. As a father, God has entrusted us with children. As an employee, God has entrusted us with a job. As an employer, God has entrusted us with employees. As a Christian, God has entrusted us with the good news of Jesus Christ.

How are we guarding, protecting, and keeping that which God has entrusted to us? Do we even view what we have in this way? I believe too many times we do not view what we have as being given by God. It is much easier to slack off if we keep things in a worldly perspective. However, as Christians we just cannot do this. Everything we have in life has been given to us by God, and the sooner we view it this way, the better we can guard and protect it.

How are you guarding that which has been entrusted to you by God? And have we passed on that trait to our sons? Not just by observation, but by instruction?

Without Delay

Third, we read that David wastes no time doing what his father had asked him to do. "Early the next morning," David was doing the job his father had given him. In 1 Samuel 17:17, Jesse had told David to "hurry to their camp," therefore, David did not hesitate. He did not find reasons to delay or delegate the job to someone else. He got up early the next morning and took care of it himself. Just think, if David had hesitated or left mid-morning, he may have arrived at camp at a different time and never heard Goliath's challenge. He may never have had the opportunity to fight the giant.

How do we react when we have a job to do? Do we respond immediately, or do we wait to see if someone else will do it, or hope it will just go away? Psalm 119:60 says, "I will hasten and not delay to obey your commands." If we believe God has entrusted us with our families, jobs, and everything we have, then we should not delay in doing our best in each role. Whether it is our job as a husband, father, employee, or Christian, we should not delay in doing what God has given us to do. This is especially critical when it comes to raising our sons in a godly manner.

JESUS' HEART

Jesus was also given a specific job to do by His Father, and He too had to answer the call. We pointed out in the last chapter that Jesus knew His power. Matthew 26:53 says that Jesus knew He could call legions of angels down from heaven, but this would not do the job. Only Jesus could do the job His father had given Him. He could not delegate it or postpone it. In John 12:27, we see that Jesus was troubled over what had to be done. But He knew the job He had been given and knew that, "it was for this very reason He came to this hour." This knowledge of the job did not make it any easier, but it did make it clear.

Like David, Jesus performed many jobs while on earth, but the main job was that of Savior. In John 12:47, Jesus says, "I did not come to judge the world, but to save it." He knew there would be a time and place for the world to be judged. However, God had sent Him to save the world. Jesus was not saying and doing what He wanted; He was doing what His Father commanded Him to do (John 12:49). As difficult as it was, Jesus knew the job His Father had given Him and knew that He was the only one who could do it.

Jesus is the "Good Shepherd," and as we saw with David, Jesus would not have left His sheep without first making sure they were taken care of. Before Jesus left the disciples, He promised to send them the Holy Spirit. In John 16:7, Jesus says, "Unless I go away, the Counselor will not come to you." Jesus knew that in order for the Holy Spirit to come, He had to leave. In Acts 2:4, we read that — just as Jesus promised — "All of them were filled with the Holy Spirit." Like every good shepherd, Jesus did not leave His sheep unattended.

Although Jesus is not here with us physically today, He has sent the Holy Spirit to be our shepherd through life. Romans 5:5 assures us that "...God has poured out his love into our hearts by the Holy Spirit, whom he has given us."

Jesus' Calling

Just as God gave Jesus a specific job and Jesse gave David a specific job, God has also given us specific jobs. We should learn from Jesus and David to act immediately. If necessary, we should take care of the job we are currently doing, then get on to what He has called us to do. Do not hesitate or try to wait for someone else to do it. Ephesians 2:10 tells us, "We are God's workmanship, created in Christ Jesus to do good works, which God prepared in advance for us to do." God has prepared these works for you, not someone else.

We have a great example of how to answer God's call in how Peter, Andrew, James, and John answered Jesus' call. Matthew 4:18-22 gives us the account of these four men becoming disciples. Jesus said, "Come follow me," and the Bible tells us that Peter and Andrew, "at once left their nets and followed him." About James and John the Bible says, "Jesus called them, and immediately they left the boat and their father and followed him."

All four men were called by Jesus to follow Him and there was no hesitation. They left their livelihoods and their families and followed Jesus. There was no hesitation, no delay, nor any excuses. They did not wait for someone else to do it. They did not remain in their comfort zones. They were willing to answer the call of Jesus immediately.

In contrast to these four men is the story of the rich young man (Matthew 19:16-22) who asked Jesus, "What must I do to inherit eternal life?" Jesus gives him the same invitation, "Come, follow me." But he was not willing to give up all he had to follow Jesus. Instead, "he went away sad." What a difference it makes in our lives when we answer Jesus' call.

Like Jesus and David, all these men had the opportunity to have their lives radically changed, but only the four answered the call. We have the same opportunity. Jeremiah 1:5 says that God knew us before we were even in our mother's wombs. Before we were even born, He set us apart to do the good works He has prepared for us. God has a plan and purpose for us to prosper (Jeremiah 29:11).

We must answer the call, though. We cannot be like the rich young man and value our worldly possessions more than being in the will of God. Sometimes it may seem impossible to answer, but God has the perfect plan for us. I am sure it was not easy for the disciples to leave all they had to follow

Jesus, and it was not easy after they made that decision. But from the perspective of eternity, it was a great decision!

Answer the Call

Centuries ago a king set out to create the greatest breed of horses the world had ever known. In his quest, he sent out his best men to find the finest horses in the known world and to bring them back. Sometime later the men returned with what they believed were the greatest horses in the whole world. The king began to train the horses himself. He taught them to respond to him every time they heard the sound of his war trumpet. After months of hard, vigorous training to the war trumpet, the king felt it was time to test the training.

The king took the horses into the desert to a place of unbearable heat. He put them in a corral on a hill overlooking a bubbling oasis of cool water only 100 yards away. He gave the horses nothing to eat or drink. The horses only had the oasis 100 yards away to look at. After a few days, it became impossible to contain the horses. They were about to destroy each other and the corral. They were desperate. The king decided it was time for the ultimate test. Were any of these horses truly be up for the challenge? Would any of them be able to answer the call?

The king ordered the gates opened and the horses went straight for the oasis. They could almost taste the water. The heat and thirst had made these once tame horses uncontrollable. The test came when the horses were within 100 feet of the life-saving water. The king blew his war trumpet. To the surprise of the king and his men, five of the horses came to a halt and returned to their master. From these five horses, we're told, the Arabian horse was bred.

Like the rich young ruler and most of the horses, not everyone is willing to answer the call. One reason is that not everyone is willing to give up all the world has to offer. We desire the water too much. We have to have it here and now; we do not trust our master. We believe we know what is best. Although we know what we should do, we just do not have the self-discipline to do it. As fathers, it is essential to build into our sons the ability to heed God's call despite the pressures of the godless culture surrounding them.

Another reason we do not answer the call is that we are not conditioned to hear it. We must be willing to go through the proper training so we can learn to recognize the voice or sound we should be listening for. There are many distracting and enticing things in the world. Just like the riches the young man had, or the water the horses wanted so badly, life is full of distractions. To overcome their pull, we must be in God's Word, be in prayer, and be in fellowship with other Christians. This will greatly enhance our ability to know what our Father is calling us to do. God's Word promises that if we search for Him, we will find Him (Jeremiah 29:13).

The world was saved from eternal death because Jesus answered His Father's call. Goliath was defeated because David answered his father's call. The modern church is what it is today because a few Christians answered their Savior's call. These men were able to answer their masters' call because they had conditioned themselves to do just that.

We too must condition ourselves to know our Mater's call. We all have the choice to answer the call or to keep running to the water or to worldly possessions. Which choice will you make?

LESSONS FROM JESSE

My wife and I took a parenting class several years ago and one of the recurring themes was the term "parenting outside the funnel." This basically means that we allow our kids too many choices and too much gray area. We often start at the large end of the funnel as parents instead of the small end. I know from playing and coaching sports, if a player is thinking instead of reacting, he is not as good. I believe it is the same for our boys. The fewer choices we can give them and the more detailed we can be with our instructions, the better they will do.

How many times do we tell our sons to do something and because we are not specific, they do not even know where to start? Then we get on them for not doing what we asked them to, when the real problem is they have no idea what we want them to do to begin with. There are many reasons for this. We are just too tired from a day at the office, or we are busy watching our television show. Whatever the reason, we need to learn to be specific when we ask kids to do a job.

The best example in our family is when it comes to picking out clothes. I just love that time. We tell the boys to get clothes out for church and they lay out gym shorts and T-shirts. Then it begins. We get on them for their choice and they stand there confused. They did exactly what we told them to; they picked out clothes. Now if we had asked them to get out their blue collared shirts and khaki shorts, it would have cut down on the confusion and also taught them what the expected attire for our particular church is.

Another classic example is when we tell the boys to put away their clothes, which have been folded and placed on the couch. It never fails that the clothes end up on their beds or the tops of their dressers. They know where the clothes are supposed to go, but there is something inside a man that thinks if clothes are inside his room then they are put away. Unless we tell our kids to put the socks in the top drawer, the shorts in the middle drawer, and the shirts in the bottom drawer, we just have to accept the bed or the top of the dresser. If we want the job done correctly, we have to be specific.

Details from Jesse

Jesse must have known that children, and especially boys, need specifics. Look at the specific directions he gives David. First, he tells him to take "this ephah of roasted grain and these ten loaves of bread for your brothers." Now that is specific. Not just any roasted grain or ten loaves, but "these." He obviously provided the grain and loaves for David to take. He does not tell his son to take some grain and some loaves. Jesse probably had the same experience picking out clothes for church as me; or maybe David was like every other boy and just could not get those clothes in the drawers without specific instructions.

Whatever the reason, Jesse makes sure David knows exactly which grain and which loaves to take to his brothers.

He then tells him to "take along these ten cheeses to the commander of their unit." Once again, look at the detail given to David. He is told which cheeses and how many. He is also told exactly to whom the cheeses are to go:

to "the commander of their unit." Jesse gives David little room for error. Jesse gives David very few choices, just a specific job with details.

Not only does Jesse tell David exactly what to take, but also what he needs to bring back. If David was like the boys of today, Jesse may have had to ask David if he needed to write this down. Jesse does not just want David to take his brothers supplies; he also wants to know how they are doing.

Jesse does not need a parenting book to know that boys do not ask questions, and they are sure not going to check on their brothers without specific instruction. Remember David is the youngest of eight boys; this is not Jesse's first rodeo.

Jesse not only tells David what to take and what to bring back, but he also tells when to take it and where to take it. In verse 17, Jesse tells David to "hurry to their camp." This little detail in the instructions causes David to get there early enough to hear Goliath, which ultimately leads to him killing Goliath. I believe God was with Jesse as he gave David these instructions, and the timing piece was possibly as critical as any of the details.

Jesse and David's culture was not condescending toward giving very specific instructions. In a day where you couldn't call to double check the instructions, it was necessary to be clearly understood. Whether you were a servant or a son, you had only one chance to find out exactly what your superior wanted you to do. Not only that, but like an ambassador, David represented his father in the front lines.

Maybe David did not know his brothers had gone off to war. He may have been out with the sheep when they left. Maybe he did know they had left or exactly where they were. Whether he knew or not, Jesse made sure David would not get lost. Jesse told him exactly where to go.

It could be like putting away clothes; boys may know which drawer the clothes belong in, but until they are told specifically where to put them, just getting them in the room is good enough.

Details from God

The Bible is full of details from God to His people. In the beginning, God told Adam which tree not to eat from, the Tree of Knowledge (Genesis 2:17). God gave Noah exact measurements for the ark he was to build (Genesis 6:15-16). Joshua received exact instructions from God on how to conquer the city of Jericho (Joshua 6:2-5). God is not one to operate in gray areas; He gives us exact instructions.

God did the same for Jesus. He sent Him at the exact time, told Him exactly what to say and how to say it. "For I did not speak of my own accord, but the Father who sent me commanded me what to say and how to say it" (John 12:49). Not only did God give Jesus a job to do, He gave Jesus the details to do the job. Jesus did not decide when, what, or how; His Father did.

Jesus did not have to decide the best time to come and save the world. His Father took care of that detail for Him. He sent Jesus at the perfect time. Jesus did not have to figure out exactly what to say to the people. God "commanded him what to say." He did not even have to get His presentation ready for the meeting. God even commanded Him "how to say it." God provided Jesus with the details to do the job.

Created to Do Good Works

We can learn some valuable lessons from how Jesse handled David and how God handled Jesus. First, we can learn that, as dads, we have to give our boys jobs to do. God created us to do good works and our boys need to learn this from an early age. We must instill a solid work ethic into our boys. We must give to them jobs that allow them to have success and failure. Too many times we do the jobs for them, instead of letting our boys gain their own valuable experiences. We must make the effort to give our boys jobs and allow them to succeed or fail. Every boy needs a job to do; that is why he was created.

Dads, we must not only give our boys jobs to do, we must also be very detailed with the job descriptions. We can learn from Jesse and God that details matter. As we saw earlier, Jesse left little room for error through the details he gave David. God did not send Jesus to earth and force Him to figure out things on His own. No, both of these fathers were very detailed in their instructions. We must also be very detailed.

Our boys do not need to be making all the decisions; they need to be doing the work. David and Jesus were told what to do. The thing they had to do on their own was the actual job. We too should be very detailed in the job description and allow our boys to do the job.

The other thing we must do for our boys is to make sure the jobs they are doing are "good works." There are many jobs our boys will become involved in, but some may not be the good works God has called us to do. Some works may seem good on the surface, but through our experiences we know they are not the good works we have been created for.

We must help our boys learn discernment in seeking good works.

Get in the Game!

Here is your opportunity to make this third chapter real in your own life...

Do Your Job: *1 Samuel 17:17-20*

17 Now Jesse said to his son David, "Take this ephah of roasted grain and these ten loaves of bread for your brothers and hurry to their camp. 18 Take along these ten cheeses to the commander of their unit. See how your brothers are and bring back some assurance from them. 19 They are with Saul and all the men of Israel in the Valley of Elah, fighting against the Philistines." 20 Early in the morning David left the flock with a shepherd, loaded up and set out, as Jesse had directed.

The Snap:

What jobs do you see David doing?

What is the job description his dad gave him?

What were David's choices? What did David do?

The Pass:

Read John 12:27, John 12:47, John 12:49

What was Jesus' job?

Who gave Jesus His job?

What choices did Jesus have? What did Jesus do?

The Catch:

Read Ephesians 2:10

What does this verse say about us?

How can we know what God is telling us to do?

Jeremiah 29:13, James 4:8

What are our choices? What will you do?

Chapter 4
Evaluate Your Situation

He reached the camp as the army was going out to its battle positions, shouting the war cry. Israel and the Philistines were drawing up their lines facing each other. David left his things with the keeper of supplies, ran to the battle lines and greeted his brothers. As he was talking with them, Goliath, the Philistine champion from Gath, stepped out from his lines and shouted his usual defiance, and David heard it. When the Israelites saw the man, they all ran from him in great fear.

David asked the men standing near him, "What will be done for the man who kills this Philistine and removes this disgrace from Israel? Who is this uncircumcised Philistine that he should defy the armies of the living God?" (1 Samuel 17:20-26)

DAVID'S HEART

One of the greatest things about college football is the excitement of game day. Each college has its own game day traditions and cheers. Whether it is a bonfire the night before or a walk through the crowd to the stadium, schools have their own unique ways of trying to get their teams ready to play. As a player, this is one of the highlights of the week: having a chance to see the passion and love in the eyes of the fans, hearing the cheers, and giving the high fives.

The fans know they will not be able to do anything on the field to help win the game, but they are convinced that if they get there early enough, yell loud enough, and jump up and down often enough, this just might be the thing their team needs to win.

One of the traditions at Auburn is called "Tiger Walk." It is the walk the team makes from the athletic dorm to the stadium on game day. Many teams have a similar event, but Auburn was one of the first, and I would dare say they have mastered it better than other schools.

During that short walk, the band, cheerleaders and fans line the streets to bring their team into the stadium. It is really hard to explain unless you have actually walked through it, but I believe that during this walk somehow the fans give players that little something extra needed to win. The cheers, the tears, the pats on the backs and high fives are so passionate. It is like your team is lining up for battle and the fans want you to know they are going with you. It is really an incredible scene.

I imagine David walked into a scene similar to this when he approached the Israelites as they were getting into battle positions and shouting their war chants (1 Samuel 17:20).

For a young man who had spent the last forty days with a bunch of sheep, this had to be exhilarating. Verse 22 lets us know that David was so excited that he "left his things with the keeper of supplies, [and] ran to the battle lines." He wanted to see what was going on. He wanted to be in the action. He may have been thinking, "I hope they don't start without me!"

When Goliath stepped out for the Philistines, David's excitement turned to confusion very quickly. The team he had come to cheer was afraid to even go on the field. His team was running in fear. They were not cheering anymore. No more high fives and pats on the back. Now instead of courage and excitement for the battle he saw fear and confusion.

David gives us a great lesson on how to handle any situation in the way he handles this confusing and potentially fearful time.

"Hear" and "See"

The Bible makes it very clear that "David heard it" when Goliath stepped out and challenged the Israelites. David did not just run for cover or get upset that his conversation with his brothers had been interrupted. No. David was in tune with what was happening. It is not as explicit whether or not David actually saw Goliath, but we can presume he did. First Samuel 17:24 says that when the Israelites saw Goliath they all ran. If David was on the front lines with his brothers, he was in position to see Goliath along with the rest of the Israelites.

In our busy schedules, there are many times we do not see what is going on around us. We get so focused on what is happening that we fail to hear what others are saying. We get very upset if we get off schedule, whether it is our life plans or our daily plans. We really do not want anything to interrupt us. But that is our problem.

Isaiah 55:8 says, "My thoughts are not your thoughts, neither are your ways my ways." If we are not hearing and seeing what is going on around us, we could miss out on an opportunity God is providing us.

Instead of going through life with blinders on, only hearing and seeing what we want to hear and see, we should be listening and looking for what God may bring our way. I do not believe David went to the battle to pick a fight, but he heard and saw a threat. The easy thing for David to do was act like he did not hear or see anything, but a man after God's own heart just can't do that. A man after God's heart is listening and looking for what God may bring next.

We need to keep our ears and eyes open for the next time God wants us to pick a fight with a giant. David was willing to hear and see what was going on around him.

"What "and "Who"

It is very interesting to read how David reacted to what he had seen and heard. He did not act right away. Instead he asked two things: what will be done for the person who does the job, and, who is this guy?

This may be the greatest example of all time of risk/reward behavior. David wanted to know what was in it for the man who took this guy down — the reward. He also wanted to know just who this guy was — the risk. Was the reward worth the risk of fighting Goliath?

We can learn a valuable lesson from David. We not only learn from what David does, but in what he does not do. Too many times we act before we have enough information to do the job correctly. We just jump right in and

47

start a fight. James 1:9 tells us to be "quick to listen and slow to speak." Instead of jumping into a situation, we should ask some questions to find out what is going on. Be quick to listen and get all the information needed for battle, if there is a battle to fight.

If David had just grabbed a sword and went to fight Goliath, he would have very likely been killed. Instead, David began to gather information and to evaluate the situation, and in the end that led to victory.

What David did and did not do are important, but of equal importance are what he said and did not say. His questions were confident questions, not scared ones. He was not questioning to get out of something; he was questioning to know what he was getting into.

Read the questions again. "What will be done for the man who kills this Philistine and removes this disgrace from Israel?" He was not questioning whether the Philistine could be killed; he already assumed that would happen.

The second question was, "Who is this uncircumcised Philistine that he should defy the armies of the living God?" Everyone else ran from this giant, but David showed no sign of intimidation in his questions. He showed that it is not a weak thing to question something, but a wise thing.

I believe it is also important to see what David did not ask. He asked what and who, not why, when or how. He was not wondering why this was happening. He did not ask when someone was going to do something about this Philistine. He did not ask how this Philistine was going to be stopped. He had confidence in the answers to each of these questions.

Too often we only ask why and how. Why is this happening to me? How am I going to handle this? We should be asking what and who. We should be more confident with our questions and understand that God has everything under control. He does not put us in situations that are beyond us (1 Corinthians 10:13). We should concern ourselves with what God wants us to do and who he wants us to help.

I believe God is about the what and who more than the why and how. Often, we need to trust God for the why and how and get busy with the what and who.

The Bible tells us that Jesus constantly evaluated what was going on around Him. Jesus was always looking for someone to heal, comfort, or teach. He was constantly seeing the crowds and hearing what was happening around Him.

Matthew 9:36 tells us that "when he saw the crowd, he had compassion on them."

Matthew 9:12 shows Jesus hearing what was going around him: "on hearing this, Jesus said..."

Jesus was very aware of what was going on around him (Matthew 12:15).

He was even sensitive to the touch of others (Matthew 9:20-22).

More great examples of Jesus hearing and seeing what was going on around Him are found in Matthew 14 (Jesus feeding the five thousand) and John 9 (Jesus healing the man born blind).

Hear and See with Compassion

The scene in Matthew 14 follows directly on the heels of Herod killing one of Jesus' close friends, John the Baptist. Matthew 14:13 says, "When Jesus heard what had happened, he withdrew to a solitary place." Jesus heard what had happened to John. He was not so busy with His own ministry that He was unable to hear what was happening around Him.

Jesus could have heard this news and sent His sympathies and continued on His mighty tour of miracles with His disciples. Instead, Jesus heard what had happened and it went deep into His soul. How we react to what we hear shows how we really hear what is said. Jesus heard what had happened and it hurt so badly that He needed some time of solitude.

There would be no solitude for Jesus, though. The end of verse 13 tells how crowds of people discovered where Jesus was and followed Him. Jesus had just heard about the death of one of His closest friends and wanted some time alone, but crowds were still all around Him. His reaction to this is a wonderful picture of who Jesus is and how He shows us to treat others.

Matthew 14:14 says, "When Jesus landed and saw a large crowd, he had compassion on them and healed their sick." Jesus was looking for solitude, but what He found was a multitude of people. Instead of reacting in anger or in selfishness, Jesus saw the people and had compassion on them.

Not only did Jesus have compassion on them, but He acted on this compassion by healing their sick — and later miraculously feeding thousands of hungry people.

Hear and Seek

John 9:35 records the miracle of Jesus healing a blind man on the Sabbath. This man was thrown out of the synagogue when he told the Jews how he had been healed. John 9:35 says, "Jesus heard that they had thrown him out." Once again we see that Jesus heard what had happened. It did not just go in one ear and out the other. Again, He could have continued on with His ministry. What more could He do for this man? He had already healed him. However, we see Jesus react to what He heard.

Verse 35 says "...and when he found him..." speaking of Jesus finding the man he had healed. Jesus went looking for this man after He had heard the man had been thrown out. Jesus did not just hear this and say how sorry He was. He did not tell His disciples to go help the man. Jesus Himself went in search of the man. He did not just hear what had happened; He reacted to what He heard.

Do we really hear what others are saying? Do we hear what is going on around us or do we conveniently ignore those things that may require us to make a choice? It is much easier not to hear everything, but that is not the example we see from Jesus. Many times when we really hear something it causes us to make a choice. It may cause us to step away from something we really want to do or go somewhere we really do not want to go. We should be more intent on hearing what is going on around us and reacting to what we hear as Jesus did.

Jesus saw the multitudes as an opportunity, not a burden. He went looking for the man who had been thrown out of the synagogue. How do we see people who need our help? Do we see them as Jesus saw the crowds? Do we go out of our way to find them? Do we have compassion on them?

Many times we may have the feeling of compassion, but then how do we react to this feeling? Jesus reacted to the need by meeting it. He had every reason to continue to focus on Himself and his ministry, but He chose to see the needs of others. This is the greatest example we could have.

What's in a Question?

Many times we view asking questions as a weakness. We are afraid we will look bad or maybe someone will think we are asking a dumb question. David ran that risk in asking the questions he asked. I am sure everyone who was at the battle knew who Goliath was and what would be done for the person who defeated him. However, this did not stop David from asking questions and gathering information.

We see this same thing from Jesus. After hearing and seeing, we read that Jesus asked questions too. Jesus' questions could have been viewed as dumb, but they had a purpose. Books have been written on the questions we are going to look at, but let's keep our focus on the fact that Jesus asked questions after He heard and saw.

John 6:1-15 is John's version of a story recorded in Matthew 14:13-21. Both men are at the same event and give us different viewpoints. John 6:5 is after Jesus had heard the news of John the Baptist and after He had seen the crowds. At the end of the verse He asks Philip, "Where shall we buy bread for these people to eat?" Now this was not an obvious question or even one that could be answered, but "he asked this only to test him, for he already had in mind what he was going to do." Like David's questions, this was a confident question. Jesus knew it could and would be done; He just wanted to see if His disciples recognized His ability to feed the people.

In John 9:35, after Jesus had heard what had happened to the blind man and went and found him, he asked, "Do you believe in the Son of Man?" Now this was a tough question. In John 9:22, we read that even the blind man's parents were scared to answer the simple question of who had opened their son's eyes. This was not a question that had an obvious answer. Jesus had not died on the cross and risen from the dead yet. People did not know what to think of Him at this time. The man's answer is exactly how I believe we would have answered, "Who is he, sir?"

Both of these questions go straight to the heart of who Jesus is and why He came. In David's situation we see him ask instead of act. He is trying to gather information so he will know the proper way to act. Jesus on the other hand gives people the chance to act in faith by asking questions. Jesus already knows the answer to the questions, but He asks us to help us understand. He is not trying to gather information but to give information.

Although they are for different reasons, we read of David and Jesus asking questions after they have heard and seen.

LESSONS FROM JESSE

We have all heard the old saying, "You have two ears and one mouth so you should listen twice as much as you speak." Well, I believe the Bible takes it a step further and says we have two ears and two eyes so we should look and listen before we speak. This is not a natural thing for us to do; therefore, we must begin teaching our boys when they are young. We need to teach them to evaluate every situation they find themselves in before they act or react.

First, we can see from the examples of David and Jesus that we must teach them to be aware of what is going on around them. Boys in general are not very sensitive to what is going on around them. This takes teaching and practice. We need to train our boys to see those around them and to hear what is being said. This is not so they will know other people's business, but so they can be aware of opportunities God may be presenting. Most of the time we only look at others and see what they can do for us. We must try to teach our boys to look at others to see what we can do for them.

Second, we must teach them to ask before they act. David asked questions after he had seen and heard Goliath. We need to teach our boys to ask, but also what to ask. David asked who and what. He had confidence in his questions. David's questions were to gather information. They were not questions of doubt or asked for reassurance. Our boys need to learn to ask the same type of questions. They need to be asking questions with confidence.

They need to be asking questions to gather information to help them know the situation. They must learn to ask the what and who questions, not the how and why ones.

We must also teach our sons to always be aware of their surroundings. Sometimes things are as they appear, but sometimes they are not. Our boys will sometimes be in places that are dangerous and they need to be able to recognize this.

We will not always be there to help our boys see when they are in a bad situation. But if we teach them to hear and see what is going on around them and they know how to ask the right questions, at least they have a chance to recognize the situation they are in. We don't need to scare our kids, but we do need to prepare them.

Get in the Game!

Here is your opportunity to make this fourth chapter real in your own life...

Evaluate Your Situation: *1 Samuel 17:23-26*

23 As he was talking with them, Goliath, the Philistine champion from Gath, stepped out from his lines and shouted his usual defiance, and David heard it. 24 When the Israelites saw the man, they all ran from him in great fear.

26 David asked the men standing near him, "What will be done for the man who kills this Philistine and removes this disgrace from Israel? Who is this uncircumcised Philistine that he should defy the armies of the living God?"

The Snap:

What's going on? Let's play ball!

What did David do?

Hear and See

How does David react?

Who and What

The Pass:

Jesus heard and saw

Matthew 14:13-14

John 9:35

Jesus asked questions

John 6:5

John 9:35

The Catch:

Read James 1:19

Read James 1:25

Chapter 5

Don't Give in to Peer Pressure

When Eliab, David's oldest brother, heard him speaking with the men, he burned with anger at him and asked, "Why have you come down here? And with whom did you leave those few sheep in the desert? I know how conceited you are and how wicked your heart is; you came down only to watch the battle."

"Now what have I done?" said David. "Can't I even speak?" He then turned away to someone else and brought up the same matter, and the men answered him as before.

What David said was overheard and reported to Saul, and Saul sent for him.

David said to Saul, "Let no one lose heart on account of this Philistine; your servant will go and fight him."

Saul replied, "You are not able to go out against this Philistine and fight him; you are only a boy, and he has been a fighting man from his youth." (1 Samuel 17:28-33)

DAVID'S HEART

The Where, How and Why of Peer Pressure and Criticism

In these verses, we read that David knew peer pressure and criticism at an early age. Life is full of people who want to see us fail. Although the term "peer pressure" is relatively new, the concept has been around since the beginning of time. Anytime we try to do what is right we will be criticized, and there will be people who try to convince us to be like everyone else.

In these verses, we see several characteristics of negative peer pressure and criticism that we can learn from. We can see where criticism can come from, the form it may take, and some reasons for it.

First, there is criticism and peer pressure from David's oldest brother, Eliab. Surely David's own brother would encourage and stand up for him. But we see here that many times criticism and peer pressure can come from those closest to us. The ones we expect to support and encourage us sometimes are the very ones who try to bring us down. We should not be surprised when we are criticized by someone who we thought would support us.

Eliab used two forms of criticism with David. First, he questioned David's motives. He asked David, "Why have you come down here?" Then later in the verse he tried to answer that question himself, "You came down here just to watch the battle." This is a popular strategy and obviously has been used for a long time. Eliab tried to shame David and make David question his own motives. He was also trying to make others question David and his motives. When we try to do what is right there will be people who try to bring us down by questioning our qualifications and motives. This is their attempt to make themselves look good at our expense.

Eliab also tried to ridicule David and question his character. He asked, "With whom did you leave those few sheep in the desert?" He's saying, remember David, you are just a little shepherd boy. I am sure this made Eliab feel good in front of the men who were standing there. He also said, "I know how conceited you are and how wicked your heart is." In other words, you are not only a little shepherd boy, but you are also a bad person. These are extremely harsh words to come from an older brother. It took strength for David to stand up to this criticism and pressure. Peer pressure does not always try to get us to do things we should not. Sometimes its aim is to get us not to do things we should.

I believe Eliab acted this way toward David because he was still upset that God had chosen David over him. First Samuel 16:13 states that David was anointed to be the next king "in the presence of his brothers." When David showed up at the battle and questioned what was going on and displayed more courage than all the men there — including his older brother — Eliab "burned with anger."

The reaction of Eliab toward Goliath for forty days and the reaction of David toward the giant in one day revealed why David had been chosen and Eliab had not. Eliab could not take being shown up by his little brother. So instead of taking on Goliath himself, he tried to take down David.

Most of the time peer pressure or criticism comes from people who are jealous of us. They want to keep us down with them. They do not want us to succeed because they are not having the same success. Eliab knew what should be done, but he did not have the courage to do it. And when his little brother showed the courage he lacked, he had to try to bring David down.

The other criticism David received came from King Saul. As if it were not enough to have his own brother blast him, David heard the king's reasons why David was not fit for the job. Sometimes it will not just be our peers who criticize, but also those in authority. How often have we had a teacher, coach, or even a parent give us reasons why we can't do something? They probably do not mean to harm us, but it still crushes our spirit.

The form of criticism King Saul used has been around for a long time. He does not question David's motives but instead questions his ability. "You are only a boy, and he has been a fighting man since his youth."

Whether it be said we are too old, too young, too small, too big, too smart, too dumb, the wrong gender or the wrong race, there will always be reasons why we cannot do something.

Instead of seeing the reasons David could do it, Saul focused on the reasons he could not.

I believe King Saul used the reason why he himself would not fight Goliath to convince David why he should not. Saul did not believe he could defeat Goliath, so how could this boy? It was King Saul's job to defend the Israelites.

Many times we will take criticism from those who should be doing what we are. The reason Saul tried to keep David from fighting Goliath was because he knew he should be the one doing it.

The bottom line: Eliab wanted to keep David down where he was; Saul attempted to keep David from doing his job.

Misunderstood

Regardless of the reasons or methods of criticism and pressure toward David, both Eliab and Saul misunderstood David. They were looking at the situation from their own perspectives. David viewed things from a totally different angle. He viewed the situation through God's eyes, whereas Eliab and Saul viewed the situation through their own eyes.

Eliab's two statements about David are way off. He said David was conceited and had a wicked heart. In 1 Samuel 16:7 God told Samuel not to consider outward appearance but to look at the heart. God knew David's heart was special. Acts 13:22 records God saying, "I have found David son of Jesse a man after my own heart." Eliab obviously misjudged the condition of David's heart.

Eliab also accused David of only coming down to watch the fight. He could not have been more wrong. The problem with Eliab's claim was very basic. Even if David had only come to see the battle, there was no battle going on! I am not sure what Eliab had been watching the previous forty days, but it certainly was not a battle, unless it was the battle to see who could hide first. Eliab was right in thinking David had come to see the Israelites defeat the Philistines; he just did not realize David was the one who was going to have to do it. David did not come to watch; he came prepared to act.

Saul also misunderstood David. Saul viewed the situation from a physical perspective. He was right in the fact that David could not fight Goliath by himself. Saul's problem was that he had not factored God into the fight. None of the Israelites could defeat Goliath on their own, but through the strength of God they could. Saul failed to see God and, as we will see later, David knew this was the reason he would win. David was only a youth, but with God he was much more.

Many times in life we too are misunderstood. We have accusations made against us that could not be farther from the truth. People do not know who we really are and what we stand for. They cannot see the situation the way we do because we view things from God's perspective.

We must realize that when we view things through God's eyes, we will be misunderstood.

How David Handled Peer Pressure and Criticism

David stared peer pressure and criticism in the eyes and conquered it. We will also have to stare peer pressure and criticism in the eyes and conquer it. David gives us a good blueprint on how to do this. It could not have been easy for him because of where the pressure and criticism came from, but David shows us how to handle it. He recognized the negative words for what they were, confronted the criticisms, turned from them, and continued on with what he knew was right.

After Eliab questioned David's motives and tried to embarrass him, David confronted his brother with his own questions and attitude. Many times when we are under this kind of intense pressure we crumble and do not know what to do or say. David answered right back by asking, "Now what have I done? Can't I even speak?" David turns it back on his brother. David knew his brother was wrong about him. When we are faced with this kind of peer pressure, it's generally best to not run from it; instead we need to confront it like David.

After David confronted his brother, the Bible says, "he then turned away to someone else." David did not continue to argue; instead he confronted Eliab and then turned away. David did not give his brother the opportunity to continue to put pressure on him. David knew his battle was not with his brother. David recognized Eliab was trying to hurt him so David did the smart thing and got away from Eliab. Remember, a major reason why Eliab was questioning David was to keep him down. David knew he had to get away from his brother and not let Eliab continue to try to bring him down.

What David does next is great. Once he confronted his brother and turned away from this peer pressure, the Bible says David brought up the original matter. He did not deviate from his initial plan. He did not let peer pressure soften his stance. He did not question his motives or his character. Instead, he focused on the same matter. I believe this shows a great deal of courage. How easy it would have been for David to temper his questions and his drive. Maybe his brother was correct. Maybe he did have the wrong motive. No, David did not let the peer pressure affect his mind. He turned and went to someone else and brought up the same matter.

When we are faced with peer pressure — and we will face it all our lives — we too can overcome it as David did. We should not be afraid to confront the peer pressure and recognize it for what it is. Then, do not continue to let the peer pressure exist; turn and get away from it. Finally, if we know what we are doing is the right thing to do, we can continue on with the same matter.

We should not let peer pressure keep us from doing what we know is the right thing to do. David gives us a great plan to handle this peer pressure.

JESUS' HEART

The Where, How and Why of Peer Pressure and Criticism

Jesus faced peer pressure and criticism while on earth just like every other person who has ever lived. He faced peer pressure from His closest friends and from people in authority as well. In Jesus' case, like David, the pressure and criticism came in many forms and for different reasons. The book of Matthew gives us examples of peer pressure from one who was close to Jesus as well as examples of criticism aimed at Jesus from the Pharisees.

Matthew 16:21-28 is the account of Jesus predicting His death for the first time and Peter's response. In verse 21 Jesus explains that He must suffer, die and be raised from the dead three days later. After He had told them this, the Bible says Peter, "took Jesus aside and began to rebuke him." As with David, we see peer pressure coming from someone close to Jesus.

Rather than question Jesus' motives and character as Eliab did David, Peter questions Jesus' judgment. Peter did not confront Jesus in front of everyone; he was not trying to embarrass Jesus or make Him look bad. Instead, Peter takes Jesus to where they were alone. Then Peter "began to rebuke" Jesus. Peter tried to convince Jesus that this could not be so. Surely Jesus was wrong. He would not have to suffer and die. There had to be another way. Peter used a form of peer pressure that is easy to fall into. It came from love and reason. This kind of pressure can be hard to resist or even recognize, but Jesus was not swayed by it.

Whereas Eliab's pressure stemmed from anger and jealousy, Peter's grew out of love and concern. He had the greatest intentions in the world. He did not want to see his Lord and friend go through pain and death. He wanted Jesus to know that he had His back. Jesus, however, knew that despite the noble intentions, Peter was wrong. Peer pressure does not always come from bad intentions. Sometimes it is disguised in love and concern, but we still must recognize it and be able to handle it.

Matthew 9:10-13 gives an account where Jesus was confronted and questioned by the Pharisees. The Pharisees were a group of spiritual leaders of Jesus' day. In these verses, Jesus was dining in Matthew's house with people the Pharisees viewed as sinful people. The Pharisees were constantly trying to find fault with Jesus and this was an opportunity for them to criticize Jesus' actions.

The Pharisees disguised their criticism in the form of a question posed to Jesus' disciples. Instead of directly confronting Jesus, the Pharisees were sneaky with their attacks. They asked the disciples, "Why does your teacher eat with tax collectors and sinners?" Notice the Pharisees made sure to distinguish that Jesus was not their teacher, but the disciples' teacher.

This question presents different variations of criticism. First, the Pharisees posed the question to the disciples possibly to cause dissention between them and Jesus. Maybe they could get Jesus' disciples to question or doubt Him. Many times when we are in leadership positions, we will not take direct criticism. Instead, the criticizer will attempt to bring us down through those we are leading. This is a very sneaky and dangerous approach that we must be aware of. When someone wants to bring down a leader, they may use those under him to do so.

The other thing the Pharisees tried to do with this question was to belittle Jesus. They made sure they phrased the question so the disciples and Jesus knew they viewed Jesus as being below them. He was not their teacher. They were possibly doing this to get into Jesus' mind as a form of intimidation. This was a crafty way of trying to put Jesus down.

The Pharisees were motivated by fear and jealousy. It is obvious that the Pharisees were trying to find fault with Jesus, or why else would they even be there to see what He was doing. They were threatened by Jesus because He was doing the job they should have been doing.

As we saw with David, when we step up to do a job someone else should be doing, that person is going to look for reasons for us not to do the job either. Criticism should be expected when we step up to do a job someone else will not do.

Misunderstood

Once again, most peer pressure and criticism come when we are misunderstood. Like David, Jesus was misunderstood by Peter and the Pharisees.

Jesus was looking at the situation through the eyes of His Father and the others were viewing the situation through the eyes of the world. Jesus recognized this difference in perspective and attempted to explain it to Peter and the Pharisees.

After Peter tried to tell Jesus he would never let Jesus suffer and die, Jesus tells Peter, "Get behind me Satan! You do not have in mind the things of God, but the things of man." Peter could not understand what Jesus was telling the disciples because he was viewing things from an earthly perspective. He was viewing things through the eyes of man.

As with David, again we see that when we view things through God's eyes we can and should expect peer pressure from those who view things through the eyes of man. And many times this pressure will come from those close to us.

The Pharisees were way off in their view of Jesus. They could not understand the things He did because they had strayed so far from what God wanted them to do. They had become more concerned with works, deeds and rituals than with following God. Jesus challenged the Pharisees to go and learn what Hosea 6:6 meant, "I desire mercy, not sacrifice."

The Pharisees were so caught up in their rituals and sacrifices that they neglected to have mercy. Jesus understood that His Father was more concerned with actions toward others than with rituals.

The Pharisees totally misunderstood what God wanted them to do, which is why they could not accept what Jesus was doing.

How Jesus Handled Peer Pressure and Criticism

We see many similarities in how David handled his situations and how Jesus handled His. Like David, Jesus also took peer pressure and criticism head on. He did not try to dodge it or run from it. He recognized it for what it was, confronted it, did not dwell on it and continued on with what He knew was the right thing to do.

"Get behind me, Satan! You are a stumbling block to me." Now that is confronting peer pressure, exclamation point and all. Jesus handled Peter about as harshly as you see Jesus handle any person or situation in the Bible. He absolutely confronted Peter and his actions. Jesus recognized that Peter's pressure was coming as an attack to keep Him from doing the will of His Father.

The Bible does not say that Jesus turned from Peter, but we do know that Peter "took Jesus aside and began to rebuke him." Therefore, we know they had walked away from the crowd for Peter to talk to Jesus. But after Jesus confronted Peter, He addressed His disciples. Well, if He and Peter had walked off from the crowd, Jesus seems to have walked away from Peter to come back to the disciples. He did not dwell with the peer pressure. He confronted it and moved on.

The Bible says that David turned and brought up the original matter. Well, Jesus did the same thing. When He turned from Peter He put His attention back on teaching the disciples. He did not water down His message or change subjects. He challenged them more powerfully than before. Jesus knew His message was from the Father and He was not going to let pressure, even from a close friend, keep Him from preaching it.

LESSONS FROM JESSE

The Where, How and Why of Peer Pressure and Criticism

The examples of David and of Jesus illustrate some crucial "Jesse" principles we need to be teaching our sons about peer pressure and criticism. They must learn that peer pressure and criticism have been around for a long time, but that it is possible to defeat them. Boys will always encounter peer pressure and criticism, but if we give them the right tools, our sons will be able to confront and conquer them.

First, we must teach our boys how to recognize pressure and criticism. As with David and Jesus, it can come from those who are close to us or from those in positions of authority. If our sons do not understand where the attacks can come from, they will have a hard time defeating them. We expect those close to us or in authority positions to be for us, but we should warn our sons that this is not always the case. They must know that peer pressure and criticism can sometimes come from the most unexpected places.

It is also very important to teach boys the different forms that negative peer pressure and criticism can take. It may be like the form Eliab used, where motives and character are attacked through questions and demeaning statements. People who lack your courage may try to tear you down by attacking your character. Or it could come from someone questioning your judgment, as Peter did with Jesus. Or people in authority may try to destroy you, like the Pharisees tried to do in attacking Jesus.

One of the most common forms of pressure can be seen in what Saul said to David. Saul tried to convince David he could not defeat Goliath by questioning David's ability. He was too young and too small. Boys will be given far more excuses as to why they cannot do something than they will be given encouragement to do it. They will be told they are too old, too young, too small, too big, too smart, too dumb, and the list goes on. As fathers, we need to warn our sons about these people and their excuses. We also need to be sure we are not part of this negative group. We should encourage our boys, not discourage them!

Finally, boys need to know why peer pressure and criticism are used. Many times these things stem from anger or jealousy. Some people do not want others to succeed because they are not succeeding. They wish they had what others had, but since they do not, they try to keep everyone down on their level. In the case of Saul and the Pharisees, the criticism stemmed from the shame or guilt of watching someone else do the job they should have been doing. These people try to place their excuse on everyone else. At other times, criticism may come from those who truly love us and are just being protective.

Peer pressure and criticism come in many shapes and sizes, but they must be recognized and dealt with head on. We cannot act like they do not exist. If we ignore negative influences and do not teach our boys about them, then these negative influences will win. However, if boys know they exist and how to recognize their attacks, then at least our sons have a chance to be a conqueror.

How to Handle Peer Pressure

Teaching our sons to understand peer pressure is only part of the job we have as fathers. The rest of the job is the hardest for our boys to do. Recognizing peer pressure is one thing; knowing what to do about it and doing it are a whole separate game. From David and Jesus we can learn some general guidelines to pass on to our sons.

The first thing we must teach them is to confront the pressure. This is not easy to do. We saw that the peer pressure David and Jesus faced came from someone close to them and from authority figures. It is hard to confront a stranger, harder to confront a family member or close friend, and even harder to confront an authority figure. But we must teach our boys to have the strength and courage to stand up to anyone who is keeping them from doing what they know is the right thing to do.

We must also teach them to turn and get away from whoever is applying the pressure. They must realize the longer they stay around that person, the harder it will be to avoid the pressure. They must follow the example of David and Jesus by getting away. They should not try to reason with the person or dwell on what they are saying. We must teach our boys that it is more than okay to walk away; it is very wise. Walking away is not always the "manly" thing to do, but it is the biblical thing to do.

David and Jesus show us there is something about persevering in doing what is right. Galatians 6:9 tells us that we will reap a reward if we do not give up on doing what is right. Boys have to learn this perseverance. It is not something that comes naturally; we must continually encourage this behavior.

We must teach them that no matter who tries to stop them, they must continue to do what they know they should.

Are You Misunderstood or Do You Misunderstand?

Are we teaching our sons to misunderstand or be misunderstood? Eliab and Saul totally misunderstood David, as Peter and the Pharisees misunderstood Jesus. David and Jesus had a different perspective than the others. David and Jesus saw things from God's perspective, while the others had a worldly viewpoint. We must teach our boys to be careful what viewpoint they take in each situation.

If they are learning to have a worldly viewpoint, then they will surely misunderstand anyone who is trying to do what God wants. God's will does not always make sense to the world. Who would have ever thought David could beat Goliath? And was Jesus out of His mind with all that nonsense about coming back from the dead? If we view these situations from a worldly perspective and do not factor in God, then we can understand why Eliab and Peter took offense.

If we are teaching our sons to have a worldly view and not factor in God, then we are creating people who will be applying the peer pressure and criticism to those trying to do what God wants. Even if it is out of good intentions, like Peter, they will become stumbling blocks. It may be a popular and easier perspective, but it is not the right perspective.

If, however, we are teaching our boys to be in God's Word, to be praying and to be hanging out with others who are doing the same, then we are teaching them to have a godly perspective. God's Word tells us in Philippians 4:8, "Whatever is true, whatever is noble, whatever is right, whatever is pure, whatever is lovely, whatever is admirable — if anything is excellent or praiseworthy — think about such things."

If we teach our sons to set their minds on these things, they will have a godly perspective. When boys have a godly perspective, they need to know they will be misunderstood by the rest of the world. They need to know they will face peer pressure and criticism because of this misunderstanding.

Get in the Game!

Here is your opportunity to make this fifth chapter real in your own life...

Don't Give into Peer Pressure: *1 Samuel 17:28-30, 33*

28 When Eliab, David's oldest brother, heard him speaking with the men, he burned with anger at him and asked, "Why have you come down here? And with whom did you leave those few sheep in the desert? I know how conceited you are and how wicked your heart is; you came down only to watch the battle."

29 "Now what have I done?" said David. "Can't I even speak?" 30 He then turned away to someone else and brought up the same matter, and the men answered him as before.

33 Saul replied, "You are not able to go out against this Philistine and fight him; you are only a boy, and he has been a fighting man from his youth."

The Snap:

Where does the peer pressure and criticism come from?   How does it come? Why does it come?

How was David misunderstood?

How did David handle the situation?

The Pass:

Read Matthew 9:10-13

Where does the pressure or criticism come from? How does it come? Why does it come?

How does Jesus handle it?

How is Jesus misunderstood?

The Catch:

How do we handle peer pressure and criticism?

Galatians 6:9

Are we going to be misunderstood or will we misunderstand?

Philippians 4:8

Chapter 6
Don't Be Afraid to Dance

What David said was overheard and reported to Saul, and Saul sent for him. David said to Saul, "Let no one lose heart on account of this Philistine; your servant will go and fight him" (1 Samuel 17:31-32)

DAVID'S HEART

Garth Brooks' 1993 song "Standing Outside the Fire" is a great ballad of courage and hope. The song is about a high school track and field Olympics in which a boy with Down's syndrome signs up to compete. But instead of signing up for the Special Olympics, he signs up for the regular event. This causes great tension between his parents. His mother supports his decision but his father fears his son will be embarrassed, when it is really the father who fears embarrassment.

The boy trains extremely hard for the event with his mother's encouragement and help. When it comes time, the boy is in the blocks and ready to race. His mom is in the stands watching him, but his dad is hiding under the stands. The race begins and the boy is off and running, and in last place. As he turns the curve, he trips and falls. As he lays there all dirty and scraped up, his coach and parents come running to him. His father tells everyone to leave him alone and encourages him to finish. The ending is an incredible scene of the boy getting up and running to the finish line with a feeling of accomplishment that cannot be described.

There is one line that Brooks repeats that is the true message of the song: "Life is not tried, it is merely survived if you're standing outside the fire."

What a great line! It is so true for most people. Most people are afraid to get into the fire. It is much safer and easier to stay outside the fire. This is as true today as it was in David's time. David, however, was not afraid to step into the fire.

Remember, when David arrived at the battle, the Israelites were taking up their positions. The only problem was that once they got into position, they would not fight. This confused David and he began to ask questions as to who this Philistine was and what would be done for the man who killed him.

Much like the father in Brooks' song, David's own brother and King Saul both tried to keep him from stepping into the fire. But David knew that, "Life is not tried, it is merely survived if you're standing outside the fire." Like the young boy in the song, David was willing to get into the fire. A man after God's own heart is not interested in merely surviving life.

Lost Hope

When David arrived, tensions were high and hope had basically been lost. For forty days Goliath had come out morning and night and "took his stand" against the Israelites, and for forty days they were "dismayed and terrified." The Israelites had no answer for Goliath. Their only response was to run and hide from the Philistine. However, after forty days they had to be wondering how much longer they would be able to hide.

About this time a kid arrives and begins to ask questions and show some courage. *Maybe this kid is our hope or, at least we can send him out to be killed instead of us,* they may have been thinking. Whatever they were thinking, they thought enough of David to send word to King Saul that there might be someone willing to fight. After forty days of being intimidated by Goliath, I am sure the Israelites were willing to try anything, even a young shepherd boy who has just shown up.

Not only had the Israelites lost hope, but their king had obviously lost hope in himself. Verse 31 says that when Saul heard about David he sent for him. They did not bring David to Saul at first; they brought his story so the king could decide if he wanted to see the youth. After hearing David's story, Saul had to be desperate to send for a boy who was not even part of his regiment. He was so desperate that he would try anyone and anything at this point. If someone was willing to fight Goliath, King Saul was willing to listen.

I love what David said to Saul in verse 32. David stood before the king, the man who should be going out to fight, and said, "Let no one lose heart on account of this Philistine." This young shepherd boy stood before the king and inadvertently called him and his army cowards by reminding the king to have courage. David did not give the Israelites an excuse; he called it like it was. They were scared of Goliath. They had lost heart and given up hope on account of this Philistine. No one was willing to get in the fire. King Saul and the Israelites knew that life could be survived if they stayed outside the fire. David, however, provided hope when he declared his willingness to step into the fire.

I'll Go and Fight

David had asked the right questions, he had confronted and dealt with peer pressure, and now he was standing before the king. You have heard the saying, "talk is cheap." David had his audience, now what would he do? Well, he does what any man after God's own heart would do; he signs up to step into the fire. David did not have to fight Goliath. It was not his job. He was just a shepherd boy who had brought supplies to his brothers.

In order to fight Goliath, David first had to be willing to go. Most times in our lives if we are going to confront a giant or any obstacle, we must be willing to go. This could be the hardest thing of all. As we see with the other Israelites, the easiest thing to do is just stay where we are. The only way they were going to fight was if the Philistines attacked and forced them to fight. And even then, most of them would have probably run. David was willing to meet Goliath. We also must be willing to go when God calls us.

Next, David was willing to fight. He had no intentions of going down into the valley to talk to Goliath. David knew that if he went into the valley he was going to have to fight. He also knew he could be killed, but he was still willing to go. We might get burned if we step into the fire, but we must be willing to go and fight.

Do we provide hope with our statements and actions, or do we need hope? David shows us that even when it seems all hope is lost and no one is willing to go and fight, one person can make a difference. Matthew 5:13-16 tells us to be the "salt and light" of the world. We are to be the "salt of the earth," but not if we run and hide and lose hope in the face of trials. The Israelites lost their saltiness when they ran and hid from Goliath. As the Bible says, they "were no longer good for anything, except to be thrown out." God could not use them since they were not willing. He would get no praise from their actions.

Once we have Jesus Christ in our lives, we have a responsibility to let our light shine. We should let our light shine so all men can see it. We are not to go and hide, but we are to be willing to stand up and let our light shine. Do we put our light on a stand or do we put it under a bowl?

David put his light on a stand for everyone to see. His light brought hope to a hopeless situation. Our light can bring hope to a lost world as well. What good is it to have a light that can help everyone see, but that is in a place no one can see? We must be willing to let our light shine and step into the fire as David did.

JESUS' HEART

Like David, Jesus also faced a hopeless situation. The world was lost because of sin. The so-called spiritual leaders of His day were more concerned with rituals than with the truth. Even God's chosen people were hopelessly under Roman rule at the time. Jesus Himself had to be willing to get into the fire if mankind was to be saved from eternal death.

The Bible has a great deal to say about hope, and one constant thing it affirms is that our hope is found only in the one true God and His Son, Jesus Christ. Lamentations 3:25-26 tells us, "The Lord is good to those whose hope is in him, to the one who seeks him; it is good to wait quietly for the salvation of the Lord." We must place our hope in God and the fact that He will provide salvation. Jeremiah 14:22 says that God is our provider and our hope should be in Him.

Jesus came to be the hope for the world. Jesus came as the promised salvation for mankind.

Where Is Jesus?

Jesus came as the hope for us all, but imagine the difficulty of believing this at the time He came. We saw in the last chapter that Jesus had to deal with being misunderstood by the spiritual leaders and even His closest friends. Finally, when His disciples do believe and are convinced Jesus is the Son of God, the promised salvation, Jesus dies and throws doubt and hopelessness back into their hearts. Luke 24:21-35 gives us an account of hope being lost, but being found again in Jesus.

As two of Jesus' followers walked down the road, a man approached them and asked what they were discussing. The men respond that they were talking about Jesus. Luke 24:21 says the men replied concerning Jesus, "But we had hoped that he was the one who was going to redeem Israel." Like the Israelites of David's time, the disciples had lost hope in the fact that Jesus had come to be the redeemer. They were confused. They had seen Jesus do miracles; He had told them and showed them He was the one. But where was He now? Jesus had been crucified and it was now the third day, the day He was to come back. Where was He? The women had gone to the tomb and did not find the body. Even some other disciples had gone and they did not see Him either. Where was Jesus? Jesus' followers were hoping He was the one, but now they could not find Him. They lost hope when they lost Jesus. Did anyone know where He was?

As the men told the stranger the story, it grew dark and they invited him to stay with them. When they sat down to eat and give thanks, verse 31 says, "Then their eyes were opened and they recognized him." Jesus had been with them the whole time. Hope was not lost. It had been right there with them the whole time; they had just not recognized it. Once they realized it was Jesus, their attitude changes. Verse 32 says, "Were not our hearts burning within us while he talked with us on the road?" It is amazing how everything changes when we have hope. Jesus had been found. Hope was restored.

Just when all hope seemed to be lost, Jesus showed up. But Jesus had really been there the entire time; the men just could not or did not recognize Him. It was the same way with the Israelites facing Goliath. Hope was with them the entire time; they just could not or did not recognize it. It took a shepherd boy to see it for them.

It is the same way in our lives. Many times we feel like a situation, or even life itself, is hopeless and we wonder where God is. The fact is He is right there with us; we just have to recognize Him. Next time you feel hopeless and think Jesus is nowhere to be found, take a step back and look around. Odds are Jesus is right there with you and you just do not recognize Him.

Like David we too can be bold in the hope that we have in Jesus. Second Corinthians 3:12 says, "Since we have such a hope, we are very bold." David's boldness came from his trust and belief in God, and according to the Bible we should have this same boldness. In Jeremiah 29:11, God promises that He has "plans to give us a hope and a future." Like the two men walking down the road, we may feel hopeless, but as long as we have a relationship with Jesus He is always walking right beside us. Do not lose heart; Jesus is with you.

"He Set His Face"

We have looked in previous chapters at the fact that Jesus understood the job He had to do. He knew His role in the salvation of the world and had to fight against the peer pressure to stay focused on His job. It is one thing to talk the talk, but a different issue to walk the walk. Jesus knew what He had to do, and He was willing to do it.

After almost three years of ministry, Jesus found Himself at the moment of truth. Luke 9:51 says, "As the time approached for him to be taken up to heaven, Jesus resolutely set out for Jerusalem." Jesus knew it was time for Him to do what He had come to do. There could be no ascension if there was no death. Jesus knew that the way back to the right hand of the Father was through the cross and He could let nothing stop Him.

Just as it was with David, the first step was Jesus' willingness to go. Jesus' ministry was in full swing at this time. He was healing the sick, raising the dead, and preaching to great numbers of people. The safe and easy thing to do would be to stay where He was. He could "merely survive" right where He was. But this was not the ultimate job God had sent Him to do and He knew it. All these things were good, but it was not his final destination. Jesus knew that in order to do what He had come for He had to go to Jerusalem.

The distractions on the journey would be great. Along the way Jesus would continue to heal the sick and preach to the lost. He sent out some of His followers to prepare the way and do good works. Momentum was building for Jesus and everything seemed wonderful. The temptation for Him to stop right where He was and soak in all the fame was great. Even as He entered the city, the people cheered Him as He rode in as a king. But Jesus knew this was not why He had come.

No, Jesus knew He had to go to Jerusalem to suffer and die. He knew the pain and agony He would go through, but He was still willing to fight. He was still willing to get into the fire. The literal translation of Luke 9:51 is that Jesus set His face toward Jerusalem. In other words, despite the desire to stay and be cheered, despite the knowledge of the suffering ahead, Jesus set His face toward the cross and allowed nothing to stop Him. Jesus was willing and ready. He knew the cost He would have to pay, but He would not be denied. Jesus was willing to go and redeem your soul and mine.

Are we willing to set our faces toward the cross and let nothing stop us? It is easy to play Christian and do only what we have to when we are around Christian friends or at church. But are we willing to go where God takes us and fight whatever fight God calls us to? It is much easier to stay out of the dance or to stand outside the fire. But that is not what God has called us to do. No, in Luke 9:23 God calls each person to "take up his cross daily and follow him." Like Jesus, we should resolutely set out for the cross and let nothing stop us.

LESSONS FROM JESSE

Raising a Bold Child

One of the greatest things we can do for our boys is to be sure they know where their hope comes from. In the stories about David and Goliath and about the men walking down the road after Jesus' death, hope had been lost. The Israelites and Saul had lost hope because of the Philistines, and the two men on the road had lost hope because Jesus had died. All of them lost hope because they did not realize where their hope came from to begin with. Hope was with them the entire time; they just could not or did not recognize it. We must teach our sons to recognize where their hope comes from.

We are never without hope if we have a personal relationship with Jesus. No matter how bad things get, there is always hope through Jesus. We must teach our sons not to rely on their circumstances, friends, or their own abilities. Instead, they must always draw their hope from Jesus. Psalm 147:10-11 tells us that God is not interested in our strength, power, or material possessions. No, "the Lord delights in those who fear him, who put their hope in his unfailing love." The only hope our sons can have that will last forever and never disappoint is hope in Jesus. We must instill this into our boys at an early age before they put their hope in anything else.

There was a reason David was so bold. There was a reason that after Jesus made Himself known to the two men they became excited. Hope is a funny thing; when we have it we can conquer anything, and when we do not have it we can be conquered by anything.

In 2 Corinthians 3:12, Paul states that, "since we have such a hope, we are very bold." If our sons have their hope in Jesus, they will have confidence to go up against a giant, or to believe that Jesus is alive. Boys can be bold if their hope is in Jesus. As fathers, it is our job to make sure our sons know where their hope comes from.

"I Hope You Dance"

We began this chapter by looking at a song, and we'll end with another song. The title of this chapter is inspired by a song sung by Lee Ann Womack called, "I Hope You Dance." This song is sung from a mother to her child. The mother is encouraging her child to take chances and live life without fear. The chorus is, "And when you get the choice to sit it out or dance, I hope you dance." Is this not what we all want for our sons? Our hope is that they will have the courage to get in the fight and not be afraid to step into the fire.

Just as with David and with Jesus, if they are going to dance, they will eventually have to get on the dance floor. It would have been easy for David to stay on the hill with his brother and the rest of the Israelites. Jesus could have easily stopped on the way to Jerusalem and enjoyed the pats on the back and avoided the suffering of the cross. But no, both of them chose to get onto the dance floor. They both chose to go where they knew God wanted them. We must be willing to let our sons go when it is their time. We must encourage them and let them go into the valley or set their faces toward Jerusalem. We cannot do this for them, they must go themselves.

We also must prepare them for the fight. David and Jesus both had to be willing to fight. As Christians, we are not going to go where God is calling us without there being a fight. Now as we know, if our hope is in Jesus, we will ultimately win, but first there will be a fight.

We will see in the next chapter that both David and Jesus had prepared themselves for this. We will also look at how we can prepare our sons to fight. But first we have to get them to go.

Our prayer for our boys should be that they will be bold and determined to do exactly what God has for their lives.

Get in the Game!

Here is your opportunity to make this sixth chapter real in your own life...

Don't Be Afraid to Dance: *1 Samuel 17:31-32*

31 What David said was overheard and reported to Saul, and Saul sent for him. 32 David said to Saul, "Let no one lose heart on account of this Philistine; your servant will go and fight him."

The Snap:

Where was hope?

How did David provide hope?

The Pass:

Read Luke 24:21-32

Where was hope?

Where was Jesus?

How was hope restored?

The Catch:

Read Luke 9:51

Read Luke 9:23

Read 2 Corinthians 3:12

Chapter 7

Get Yourself Ready!

But David said to Saul, "Your servant has been keeping his father's sheep. When a lion or a bear came and carried off a sheep from the flock, I went after it, struck it, and rescued the sheep from its mouth. When it turned on me, I seized it by its hair, struck it and killed it. Your servant has killed both the lion and the bear; this uncircumcised Philistine will be like one of them, because he has defied the armies of the living God. The LORD who delivered me from the paw of the lion and the paw of the bear will deliver me from the hand of this Philistine" (1 Samuel 17:34-37).

DAVID'S HEART

In the mid 1990s, Nike ran an ad campaign that featured athletes preparing themselves during the off-season for their sports. Each commercial featured an athlete doing something out of the ordinary and a little crazy, but you knew what they were training for. At least three different commercials aired.

One featured Jerome Bettis, a big bruising running back for the Pittsburgh Steelers. In the commercial, Bettis throws himself down a wooded hill and rolls all the way to the bottom. On the way down he hits trees, rocks and whatever else is in the way. Once he is stopped at the bottom by hitting another tree, he gets up, shakes himself off and turns and runs back up the hill. As he does, the words "What are you getting ready for?" appear onscreen. Jerome Bettis was getting ready for another tough, bruising, and physical football season. He knew what was ahead of him.

Picabo Street was featured in another commercial. Street is a downhill skier who had broken her leg in a bad crash. In the commercial, she is in the hospital in a wheelchair with her leg in a cast. As she wheels down the hall, another person comes around the corner in a wheelchair and they bump into each other. From there they race down the hall and Street goes out the door as if crossing the finish line. As she goes through the doors the words, "What are you getting ready for?" come onscreen. She knew the training she would have to endure to get back in competitive form.

The funniest commercial starred a hockey player rollerblading through New York City. As he skates down the sidewalks, he has to dodge people, benches, signs and many other obstacles. Then he approaches an elderly lady looking through a store window. As he passes by, he body-checks her into the window and you see her face pinned against the glass with slobber coming out of her mouth. Once again, as the lady slides down the window and the hockey player zooms off, the words "What are you getting ready for?" flash across the screen.

In the commercials, the athletes knew what they were training for. They knew the exact way to get ready for their particular sport. We are not always that fortunate. Sometimes we know "what we are getting ready for" and sometimes we do not. But one thing we can know is that we must always be getting ready for whatever we may face down the road. David had no idea that he was preparing to fight a giant while he was tending the sheep, but he prepared anyway.

Keeping His Father's Sheep

When David told King Saul not to lose hope because he would go and fight (verse 32), there was a reason David could say that with such confidence. David knew what he had been doing while no one else was watching. David knew he had been preparing for what was to come. He knew he had already done the things necessary for him to defeat the giant. He had killed both a lion and a bear. Although keeping sheep seemed like a dull and unrewarding job compared to going off to battle, David had not taken the job for granted.

Keeping the sheep meant protecting them from whatever danger came along. David said that when the lion and bear came and took the sheep, he "went after it." if you thought the training in the Nike commercials was difficult, the training David had was even more intense! I can just see the shepherd boy running after the lion and the bear. Jumping over rocks and dodging bushes, sling whirling over his head ready to launch stones. Now that was serious training. Nike should do a commercial featuring David!

David said he went after the lion and the bear, but there is no way he could run them down. This makes me wonder if he used his sling and stones to slow them down. Somehow he had to get their attention and force them to turn on him. That kind of skill and accuracy would have taken a lot of practice. I can imagine David out in the desert, sifting through stones and picking out ones to practice with. I can see him setting up targets all around his flock for target practice. Maybe he found that certain size stones were really good at short distances and others were better for longer distances. Or that certain shaped stones were more accurate than others. I am not sure exactly how he prepared himself, but I do know he was prepared.

Not only did he go after the lion and the bear, but he took them on to rescue his sheep. David said he grabbed the lion and bear by the hair, struck and killed them. We will see at the end of the story how valuable this training on finishing the job would be. David prepared himself to do the job, not even knowing what the job would be.

Every Sheep Mattered

Notice David said that when a lion or bear carried off a sheep, just one, from the flock, he went after it. He did not go after the lion or the bear, he went after the sheep. He had a whole flock; why would he be so worried about a single sheep? The reason is simple; the shepherd was responsible for every sheep. It was not good enough to come back with 95 percent of the flock. It was only acceptable to have 100 percent. David knew this, and he knew he had to do whatever it took to protect every sheep.

We must be careful not to get caught up with the lion or the bear, but to remember that it is about the sheep. We must be focused on what we are supposed to do and not get caught up in battles or struggles that do not belong to us. David was willing to do what he had to in order to protect the sheep, but he did not go looking for a fight with a lion and a bear. There will be times when we have to take on the lion and the bear, but we should be sure it is for the right reasons. David knew every sheep mattered, and that was the reason to take on the lion and bear.

This is great imagery for what Jesus did for us. It was just one sheep, but every sheep was important to David. We are the same to Jesus. We are just one person, but we are all important to Jesus. David cared about the sheep so much he was willing to die for just one of them. Jesus cares for us so much that He did die for each of us. We were like the sheep in the jaws of death, but Jesus came to save us from this death. And when death turned on Him, He took it on and conquered it for us. Jesus was more concerned with our eternal salvation than with simply conquering death.

Lions and Bears

We will all encounter lions and bears in our lives and when that time comes, we must be willing to face them. As we saw earlier, David did not go in search of lions and bears. But he did know what he was willing to fight for. He was willing to fight for each and every sheep. I wonder what David would have done to a lion or bear if they took some of his food. Would he have gone after them for that? I do not know, but I do know he was willing to go after them for one sheep.

We should prioritize things in our lives so that we know when it is worth going after the lion or bear. Some things are definitely worth fighting for, but some things are not. Sometimes we get the two mixed up and fight when we should not and let the things we should fight for get away. When we prioritize things beforehand, we can know what is worth the fight and what is not.

It is also important to know that God puts lions and bears in our lives to prepare us for challenges down the road. Many times we see the lions and bears and gripe. Instead we should praise God for them and use them to prepare ourselves for the future. James 1:2-4 encourages us to "consider it pure joy" whenever these lions and bears attack. Just as wild animals came into David's life to prepare him for Goliath, trials come into our lives so we "may be mature and complete."

David also showed us how to defeat these lions and bears. In verse 37, he declared that the "Lord delivered him from the paw of the lion and the paw of the bear." David knew where his source of strength came from, but he still had to go and fight. We cannot assume God will make everything fine, but through His power and might we can overcome our lions and bears. Romans 8:37 assures us we are more than conquerors through Jesus. We can defeat the lions and the bears if we use His strength.

Without the lion and the bear, David might not have been able to defeat Goliath. Without the lion and the bear, he may not have had the confidence to go and fight the giant. He needed the lion and the bear to prepare him for what God had in his future. He had no idea how important this training would be. He did know that every sheep was worth fighting for and that with God's strength he could defeat the lion and the bear.

We also must be willing to face the lions and the bears in our lives. God has placed them there for a reason, and if we choose not to fight them we may not be ready for what God has planned for our future. We can know that God will provide the strength for us, but we must be willing to go after the stolen sheep. Praise God the next time a lion or bear comes and takes one of your sheep, and then call on Him to give you strength as you go after it.

JESUS' HEART

Very little is known about Jesus' childhood and upbringing. There are only a few verses that give us insight into this part of his life. Two of these verses are found in Luke. They indicate that Jesus had to prepare himself for what was to come. In these verses, we learn that Jesus grew physically, mentally, spiritually and socially. He would face much more than just a giant during His life, so He needed to be prepared in all areas.

Luke 2:40 tells us that as a child Jesus "grew and became strong." Jesus had to grow as any young boy would have to grow. He did not come into the world a fully grown man ready to work miracles. He had to go through growing pains and puberty just like all other boys. I am sure His voice cracked when He talked and He even had zits. He would face physical challenges in His future, so being physically prepared would be very important.

We read in this verse that Jesus was filled with wisdom. Luke 2:52 adds that Jesus "grew in wisdom." Both these verses show that Jesus did not come to earth full of wisdom; He had to grow in this area. How this worked is hard to comprehend. Jesus was with God from before the beginning of time and I am sure He knew all, but when He became human He became totally human and had to have a human mind. He had to prepare himself for life just like anyone else. Therefore, He had to grow in wisdom. He would need the experiences and knowledge of His youth to accomplish all God had for Him to do.

We also see that Jesus had to grow in "favor of God" as Luke 2:52 says. Luke 2:40 says "the grace of God was upon him." We know that Jesus had to prepare Himself to be close to God. He would have to stay close to God throughout His ministry to be successful. We also get a glimpse of this preparation in the verses between Luke 2:40 and 52. Here we read that as a young boy Jesus went into the temple to be in His Father's house. Jesus had to prepare Himself spiritually to remain close to the Father.

Jesus also grew "in favor of men." As we saw earlier, Jesus came to earth to save His sheep. He did not come to fight Satan or to conquer death for the fun of it. He came to save every sheep. His whole reason for becoming a man was for the people. Jesus would have to prepare Himself to handle people while He was here. For this reason, He would have to prepare Himself to have favor with man.

During His first thirty years on earth, Jesus was preparing for His three years of ministry. Luke 2:40 tells about when He was twelve, and Luke 2:52 provides the only details we have for the next eighteen years. But in both verses, at both times, we read that Jesus was preparing for what was to come. He knew what He was preparing for and knew how difficult it would be. This gives us all the more reason to prepare ourselves for what God has in our futures. Jesus paid attention to the details and did not go into His ministry without being prepared.

Jesus' Lion and Bear

The final preparation before Jesus began His ministry could definitely be considered a lion and a bear. All the gospels except John record this final preparation. It would be against the very one He had been sent to defeat. The very one who had the sheep in his mouth ready to devour. Jesus' final preparation would come from the devil himself. Jesus would have to face the very one who brought sin into the world through Adam and Eve. Jesus had been preparing for this moment and now it was time to put His preparation into action.

Just as David did not go looking for the lion and the bear, Jesus did not go looking for the devil. The Bible tells us that the Spirit led Jesus into the desert to be tempted. God knew that David needed a lion and a bear; He knew Jesus needed to be tempted by the devil—and overcome. Jesus did not go looking for temptation, but He would use this temptation to prepare for God's calling. We also read in Matthew 4:3, "The tempter came to him." We can have confidence that God will supply the preparation we need. We can also have confidence from 1 Corinthians 10:13 that God will not allow us to be tempted beyond what we can bear, and that He will give us a way out of temptation. This includes handling the lion and bear.

In Jesus' temptation, we see how He used all the preparation He had undergone the first thirty years of His life. Remember that Luke 2:52 said Jesus grew in wisdom and stature as well as spiritually and socially. We read that He was tempted in all these areas and was able to use His preparation to overcome the temptation. God also equips us with exactly what we need to overcome the lions and bears in our lives.

The first way the devil tempted Jesus was mentally. The devil tried to make Jesus doubt who He was with the comment, "If you are the son of God." The devil knew if he could make Jesus doubt who He truly was, he could make Jesus doubt what He believed. Jesus had prepared himself to be mentally strong. He had grown in wisdom. He used His life experiences and his relationship with the Father to know who He was. The devil failed to make Jesus doubt Himself or question what He believed.

Jesus had been in the desert forty days and had eaten nothing during that time. Matthew 4:2 says, "After fasting forty days and forty nights, he was hungry." The devil went straight to this physical need with his temptation for Jesus to "turn these stones into bread." There does not seem to be anything wrong with this. Jesus was hungry and this would satisfy his physical need. However, Jesus had come to the desert to fast and rely on God for His every need. Jesus answered this temptation with the scripture, "Man does not eat on bread alone, but on every word that comes from the mouth of God."

We too are faced with many physical temptations that at first can seem harmless. Alcohol, illegal drugs, premarital sex, and many other sins can start out with the simple act of satisfying a physical need. Jesus had prepared Himself physically to handle these situations. We must have the physical discipline to avoid sensual temptations. It took Jesus' preparation to handle this physical temptation and it will take us the same type of preparation. Like Jesus, we must rely on God, not the world, to be our physical provider. Just as with David and the lion and bear, God will also deliver us if we allow Him too.

The devil next tempted Jesus to prove God's power and love. However, Jesus had grown in His knowledge and favor with God to where He knew He did not have to prove or test God. Once more He answered with scripture, saying, "Do not put the Lord your God to the test." Jesus knew God and His vast love and power. He did not need to test God in these matters. If Jesus had not grown close to God in His preparation, He may not have had the same confidence in God. We need to be sure we are growing close to God so we will know His love and power in our lives.

The final temptation was perhaps the hardest of all. The devil took Jesus up to a high mountain, showed Him all the kingdoms of the world and offered Him the thing we all long for – power. Who does not want to have fame, power and money? There it all was right in front of Jesus, the fame, power and riches of the world. All He had to do was bow down and worship the devil. Jesus had gained favor with God and man in His thirty years of preparation, and He knew this quick fix could not substitute for the years of training He had gone through. He answered the devil, "Worship the Lord your God and serve him only."

This temptation has snared many men. The chance to have power and fame is sometimes just too hard to pass up. Many times we do not even realize we are worshiping our jobs or our material things. We get so caught up in the power and fame that we lose ourselves. We must be grounded in our training to know that God will provide our power and fame. Our favor with man must be based on our favor with God. In His thirty years of preparation, Jesus had gained favor from God and man. Jesus did not let the offer of a quick fix from the devil ruin a reputation He had been building His whole life.

Like Jesus and David, we too will face our lions and bears. Whether it is through trials or temptations, we will go through things that will challenge us in all areas. We must remember that these trials and temptations are meant to make us stronger. The Bible tells us that God will give us all we need to handle these situations. We should consider trials and temptations as training, or as a way to sharpen our skills. If we have prepared ourselves and continue to prepare ourselves, we will be ready for whatever God calls us to do.

LESSONS FROM JESSE

In Jeremiah 1:17 God told Jeremiah, "Get yourself ready!" God had a plan for Jeremiah's life and he was going to have to prepare himself for what was to come. I believe we can apply this lesson as fathers. We need to issue the same challenge to our sons, get yourself ready! God has a plan for our sons' lives and we need to make sure they prepare themselves for God's calling. I believe that is what Jesse was doing with David. Jesse made David get himself ready before he faced Goliath.

There are many lessons we can learn from Jesse through the life of David. The first one is that we have to allow our boys to tend the sheep. Jesse did not hire someone else to tend the sheep. The Bible does not say he allowed David just to help. No, Jesse made David tend the sheep. We need to give our boys jobs to help them prepare for life's challenges. It was in the field with the sheep that David discovered how strong he was. He became aware of his strengths and weaknesses there. He learned many valuable lessons about himself because Jesse made him tend the sheep.

Jesse was seemingly very demanding and I believe he had instilled discipline and pride into David. When the lion and the bear came and took sheep, David went after them. He knew his dad expected his best. Jesse would not settle for 95 percent of the sheep being saved; he expected David to take care of all the sheep. This responsibility is something we need to teach our boys. They need to know and experience doing something 100 percent. We should not accept them giving us 90 percent. This does not mean our boys will never make mistakes; however, it does mean we must attempt to instill in them a pride in doing a job to their best ability. God did not expect Jesus to overcome two of the three temptations, He expected Him to overcome them all.

David also conquered a lion and a bear while in the field with those sheep. How many times do the lions and bears come into our boys lives and we are there to run them off? We have to let our boys kill the lion and the bear on their own if we expect them to take on the giant. Jesse would not be there when David faced Goliath, and we will not always be there when our boys come up against giants. If we have not allowed them to take on the lion and the bear, they will not be able to take on the giant. God had prepared Jesus for His confrontation with the devil, which is why He allowed Jesus to be led into the desert. If we properly equip and train our boys before we send them into the field to tend the sheep, we will be able to let them take on the lion and the bear, which will prepare them for the giant.

David and Jesus showed they had learned not to chase after a fight, and also knew which fights were worth fighting. We need to teach our boys not to go looking for challenges, but to recognize the ones God places in front of them. God will provide our boys the necessary trials and temptations they need to prepare them for his calling. He will also provide them with the strength and knowledge to handle each of these situations. The key is for our boys to be close enough to God to call on His strength and power.

Whether or not we realize it, we are preparing our boys for something – either success or failure. As fathers, we can learn great lessons from God and Jesse that will help us give our boys a chance at success. The question is, what are we training them for? If someone followed us and our boys for a day, a week, a month, or even a year, what would they say we are getting ready for? The Bible teaches that preparation is the key to victory.

Get in the Game!

Here is your opportunity to make this seventh chapter real in your own life...

Get Yourself Ready! *1 Samuel 17:34-37*

34 But David said to Saul, "Your servant has been keeping his father's sheep. When a lion or a bear came and carried off a sheep from the flock, 35 I went after it, struck it, and rescued the sheep from its mouth. When it turned on me, I seized it by its hair, struck it and killed it. 36 Your servant has killed both the lion and the bear; this uncircumcised Philistine will be like one of them, because he has defied the armies of the living God. 37 The LORD who delivered me from the paw of the lion and the paw of the bear will deliver me from the hand of this Philistine."

The Snap:

Flashback to doing his job.

David's training.

Lions and Bears – every sheep mattered.

The Pass:

Read Luke 2:40

Read Luke 2:52

What do these verses tell us about Jesus as he grew up?

How did Jesus grow?

Read Matthew 4:1-11 about Jesus' lions and bears

The Catch:

Read James 1:2-4, Romans 8:28

Read Philippians 4:13, 1 Corinthians 10:13

Read Jeremiah 1:17

Chapter 8
Do What You Do

Then Saul dressed David in his own tunic. He put a coat of armor on him and a bronze helmet on his head. David fastened on his sword over the tunic and tried walking around, because he was not used to them. "I cannot go in these," he said to Saul, "because I am not used to them." So he took them off. Then he took his staff in his hand, chose five smooth stones from the stream, put them in the pouch of his shepherd's bag and, with his sling in his hand, approached the Philistine (1 Samuel 17:38-40).

DAVID'S HEART

Boxes Everywhere

How many times in life do other people try to tell you how you should do something? It seems like in our modern world this would not happen as often. However, it is just as bad today as it has ever been. Although we have more freedom and more choices than ever, we seem to have fewer choices and freedom. If you want to be a doctor, you have to go to this school. If you want to be an athlete, you have to be this big. If you want to be a model, you can only weigh this much. We live in a world full of boxes. It seems as though there is a box for everything, and if we try to do something out of the box, people look at us strangely or tell us it cannot be done.

Well, in David's time, if you were going to fight someone, you had to be a warrior and fight with swords and wear armor. But David was not this kind of warrior, and this confused everyone. Many times people can have the best intentions, but in reality they are hindering more than helping. Some people believe they have the only way things can be done. But the reality is they only know the way they would do it. Some people have a hard time thinking outside the box because they have always been inside it.

This was apparently the case with Saul and David. After Saul finally agreed to let David fight Goliath, he tried to send the youth out as he would go. The Bible says Saul dressed David in "his own tunic." He also put a coat of armor and a helmet on David. Now can you imagine this young shepherd boy with all this gear on him? It reminds me of the movie *Big* when Tom Hanks reverts from being a grown man to a boy. When this change happens, he is still wearing the suit he had on as a man and it absolutely swallows him up. I can just see David standing there with the sleeves so long he cannot even see his hands. The helmet was hanging over his eyes so he cannot even see in front of him. Now this is the picture of a mighty warrior, or is it?

Then to add to the outfit, a sword was put on David. I am sure the weapon was about as big as David himself. How would you expect a youth to put on a large man's clothes and armor and go fight someone? Because that is the only way they knew how to do it. That was the box you had to be in to fight. Saul was trying to make David into a warrior the only way he knew how. That was with a sword and body armor. Was there any other way?

We have to be careful of two things. First, we cannot be like Saul and think there is only one way to do something. We must be willing to let others be themselves. If someone else is doing a job, be careful of telling them how to do it. You may give them advise or recommendations, but remember, if you want it done your exact way, then you had better do it yourself. Just because you are comfortable doing something one way does not mean everybody is comfortable with that way. Make sure you are willing to look outside the box and willing to let other people do things the way they feel most comfortable. The bottom line was that someone had to defeat the giant; it really did not matter how it was done.

The second thing we need to be careful of is not to let other people change who we are. David was not a warrior; he was a shepherd. He had not trained in the armor or with the sword. This was the way Saul had trained and the way he would have fought the giant; it did not mean it was the only way. Do not be afraid to trust your training. It is okay to do like David did and try on the clothes or look at other suggestions, but in the end we must do it the way we know we can get the job done.

David gave it a try. He put on Saul's tunic, the armor, the helmet, the sword and even walked around in them. He was not afraid to give it a try. But this just was not who David was. He was not used to all this equipment. It was a good thought with good intentions, but it was just not the right fit for David. After all, it was Saul's tunic. This was a case of life and death, and David knew that he could not fight in all that armor.

So He Took Them Off

The end of verse 39 says, "So he took them off." David was not afraid to go against what others thought, even a king. Saul wanted to dress him up in armor to fight Goliath, but David knew this was not the best thing for him. David was not afraid to be his own person and do things his own way. We have already seen David stand up to peer pressure and criticism; once again we see him standing up for himself. He was sure he could defeat Goliath, and he was equally sure he could not do it the way Saul expected. He had to take off someone else's armor and do what he knew he could do.

Many times in life we have to do the same thing. People place expectations or restrictions on us. They want us to wear armor we are not used to. Sometimes we may have to do like David and take off what others are trying to put on us. These things might be placed on us with the correct motives, but they just do not fit. We must not let people put us in a box. We must not be afraid to try different things, but like David, we should make sure they fit us before we go fight a giant.

Five Smooth Stones and His Sling in Hand

I can just see David going down to the stream to choose his stones. He had his staff in one hand and his sling in the other. He was still a bit confused from trying on Saul's armor. He may have still been readjusting his own clothes. He looked out in front of him and could see Goliath staring back.

As he squatted down by the stream, I can see David trying to gauge just how tall Goliath was. Maybe he tried to see just how far the battle lines were from each other. He had to figure out how far he would have to throw the stone. It had to be big enough to kill Goliath, but it could not be too big or he would lose his accuracy. He probably even thought back to his time tending the sheep and what kind of stones he had used on the lion and the bear. One thing we can be certain of: David did not just grab some stones and put them in his bag. The Bible is specific with the fact that David chose five stones.

There have been many explanations as to why David chose five stones and I have my own thoughts. I believe he was preparing for many scenarios. He had to have stones he could throw from different distances. He knew the size and shape he needed for each throw. There was not a one-size-fits-all stone. Not knowing the exact throw he would have to make, he chose a stone for each possibility. He might only get one throw, so he had better make it count. He might not get a second chance.

The sling in his hand was like a part of him. It was who he was and it gave him all the confidence in the world walking out to face the giant with that sling in his hand. He also knew the stones. He knew how each one would fly out of that sling. I love the thought of David squatting at the stream with both eyes on Goliath, his sling in one hand and feeling for just the right stones with the other. Now this was who he was. He was in his element with his sling in hand choosing stones.

As he picked his fifth and final stone, David stood and placed it in his bag with his eyes still fixed on Goliath. He was ready now. He had what he needed. As Goliath approached, David began to walk toward the giant with one hand still in his bag ready to pick the right stone and the other hand clutching his sling.

We also have many choices in life. But too often, instead of taking our time and choosing the best stones, we just grab whatever we come to first and take off. We can learn a valuable lesson from David – that while we may have our eyes on the giant, we still have to take time to select what we need to defeat him. Do we spend the proper amount of time with God to prepare our arsenal for the challenges we will face? Or do we think any old stone will work? Like Saul, the world thinks it has just the right armor and sword for us. Only God can provide all we need to defeat the giants we face, but we have to make the right choices and be sure we have what we need.

Ephesians 6:13 says, "Therefore put on the full armor of God, so that when the day of evil comes, you may be able to stand your ground." Like David, we must choose the proper stones or armor of God to stand against all the devil throws at us. We must strap on the belt of truth and the breastplate of righteousness. We must tie our shoes with peace and protect our hearts with the shield of faith. On our head we must wear the helmet of salvation, and in our hand carry the sword of the Spirit. While we are equipping ourselves or choosing the stones, we must keep our eyes on the enemy as David did.

David knew he must use his sling and the proper stone to kill Goliath. We too know what it will take to stand up against the devil. David was willing to stand up and do what he had to. Are we willing to stand up and do what we must do? Will we be disciplined enough to put on the full armor of God, or will we let the world dress us in its armor? Will we settle for grabbing the first stones we find? We know the way to victory, but we must choose to take our slings in hand and choose the right stones.

JESUS' HEART

As with David, people also attempted to put Jesus in boxes. It has been human nature from the beginning of time to place people in boxes. It was no different for Jesus than it was for David, or than it is for us. Boxes have existed forever, and I am sure will exist until Jesus returns. If He could not escape being put into a box, what makes us think we will be able to escape them?

As we saw with David, many times those closest to us will be the ones who put us in boxes. In the Gospel of Mark we see two instances where Jesus' family and friends put Him into boxes. In Mark 3:21, Jesus' family came to Jesus and claimed He was out of His mind. Whether they were trying to protect Him or themselves, they placed Jesus in the box of being a crazy man. They could not understand how He could be performing these miracles. They reasoned that He must have been out of His mind or possessed.

In Mark 6:3, Jesus returned to His hometown and began to teach. The people heard Him and were amazed at His teaching, and they began to question where He had gained all this knowledge. Instead of hearing and believing, they returned Jesus to the box they had seen Him in while He was growing up. How could He know these things? After all, He was only a carpenter. They knew Jesus' family and where He came from, and they refused to believe He was any better than they were. Therefore, they placed Him in the box that made them feel more comfortable.

As Jesus' ministry grew and He continued to teach and do miracles, His boxes began to change. In Mark 8:29, Jesus asks Peter who the people said He was. Peter reported that some said He was John the Baptist, others thought He was Elijah, and still others said He was a prophet of old. People did not know who Jesus was, but it was convenient for them to place Him in boxes they were familiar with. There was not another box to put Jesus in, and they were not capable of creating a new box.

After Jesus had been crucified, His followers were brokenhearted. While He was on earth, most of his followers had placed Jesus into the box of earthly ruler and king. They believed His kingdom would be a political one on earth. In Luke 24:21, as two of Jesus' followers walked down the road to Emmaus, they said, "But we had hoped that he was the one who was going to redeem Israel." They had hoped Jesus would redeem them now. They could not understand that He had really come to redeem the world for eternity.

What box have you placed Jesus in? Do you see Jesus as being out of His mind? Do you see Him as being just another man or prophet? Are you hoping Jesus will give you earthly success, or do you see Him for who He really is, the Savior of the world? Is Jesus the one who gives you strength to do everything as Philippians 4:13 says?

I challenge you to take Jesus out of the box and discover His true power. Search the Bible for the true power of Jesus Christ. He is bigger than any box. I hope you will discover the Jesus of Ephesians 3:20, who "is able to do immeasurably more than all we ask or imagine."

Put Your Towel On

During His life on earth, people did not know what to think of Jesus. As we just saw, some called Him crazy, some thought He was just another prophet, while others thought He was going to be an earthly king. It is impossible to sum up what Jesus was in just one word, but I believe He knew who He was. There is one story in the Bible that shows Jesus doing what He knew how to do, and that was to serve. As Jesus said in Matthew 20:28, "The son of Man did not come to be served, but to serve, and give his life as a ransom for many," Jesus knew what He did best.

John chapter 13 tells the story of Jesus washing the disciples' feet. Now it was not normal for the host of a dinner, much less the "Teacher" or "Lord," to be the one to wash the feet of the guests. However, as Jesus explained to His disciples, He did this to set the example of service for them. He showed them through His actions what they were to do for each other, and what they would do later for the world. Jesus was demonstrating what He said was the second greatest commandment: "Love your neighbor as yourself."

As the meal was being served, Jesus got up from the table and took off His outer garment. I imagine His disciples looked at Him about the same way the Israelites looked at David when he went to meet the giant with just his staff and sling. They had to think, what are you doing Jesus? Have you lost your mind? Then Jesus really freaked them out when He picked up a towel and wrapped it around His waist. They knew that could only mean one thing; He was going to wash their feet.

I think the Israelites were not sure if David was really going to fight Goliath, but when he went to the stream to pick his stones, they knew he was really going to do it. The disciples probably had the same reaction. When Jesus first got up, they were unsure what He was doing, but when He put on the towel, they knew what He intended to do.

John 13 tells us that Jesus knew He had been given all power from God. He knew He was returning to His rightful place next to the Father. However, He also knew what He had to do first. He had to give His disciples this example, and although they may not understand it now, later they would see the significance. Peter would be the one who tried to stop Jesus from washing his feet, and he would be the one Jesus would later tell to "feed my sheep." His disciples were going to have to give so much of themselves to spread the good news that they had to experience Jesus giving of Himself in order to have a perfect example to follow.

Are we willing to put on a towel and follow Jesus' example? Are we willing to serve as Jesus served? This is what we have been called to do – serve. Galatians 5:13 commands us to "Serve one another in love." Ephesians 6:7 tells us to "Serve wholeheartedly, as if you were serving the Lord, not men." First Peter 4:10 says to "Use whatever gift you have received to serve others."

The Bible is very clear that we are to serve others. Now, are we willing to put on a towel, follow Jesus' example and start serving? David had a sling in his hand and Jesus had a towel around his waist, but they were both doing what they did best.

LESSONS FROM JESSE

When Samuel came to Jesse to pick one of his sons as the next king, they had to step outside the box. I am not sure either of them was quite ready to step outside the box like they did. However, both Samuel and Jesse were willing to follow God, even if that took them out of their normal comfort zones. This is the example we should be setting for our boys. We must be willing to follow God even if it takes us out of our boxes.

When Samuel first saw Eliab, Jesse's oldest son, he thought this had to be the one the Lord had chosen. This was only logical. During this time, the firstborn was the most important. He would receive a double portion of the inheritance. He had top priority in the family, and he would be the heir to the throne if he was the king's son. It made sense that Samuel would think Jesse's oldest son would be the chosen one. In fact, Jesse didn't even seem to consider David as a legitimate choice for Israel's next king. He was, after all, the last son and a very young man. This is probably why Jesse didn't call David in from the fields when Samuel came to anoint one of his sons as king.

I have to believe that Eliab also looked the part. It says that when Samuel saw Eliab, he thought this would be the one. At this time, looks were very important to the people. Saul himself was said to be an impressive man without equal and a head taller than anyone else. Samuel and Jesse must have thought that the next king would fit into the same box as Saul. He must have the outward appearance of a king. However, God told Samuel that although man looks at the outward appearance, He looks at the heart.

Not only did they have to go outside the lineage box, now they had to go outside the appearance box. God was really testing Samuel and Jesse. Would they continue to follow Him or would they use the boxes the world had created? Well, obviously they went outside the box with God. This had to be a great example for David. His dad was willing to step outside of the boxes the world had created and follow God. No wonder David was able to step outside the box and face Goliath with just a sling and five stones.

Are we willing to be the example to our boys? It is easy to go through life in the boxes the world has created. The problem is that these boxes were created by men, not God. We must be willing to follow God even if that means stepping outside the box.

Jesse was willing to go against everything the world held to be true. He went outside the social norm of choosing the firstborn, and he went outside the box of appearance. The box he did stay in was the "box" of following God.

Carry Your Own Load

David realized something very important as he was trying on King Saul's armor. David realized that it was not Saul going out to fight Goliath, it was David. Why would David try to be Saul? We must teach our boys to carry their own load and not someone else's. Galatians 6 tells us to examine our own work and make sure we do a good job of what we are supposed to do. It tells us not to compare ourselves to others but to carry our own load.

I believe Jesse taught David this principle. Jesse taught his son to focus on what he was doing or had to do and not on what others were doing. Too many times we become occupied with what the person down the street is doing, or what our co-worker is doing. Our boys get caught up in what the other boys at school or on their teammates are doing. We should provide an example of not concerning ourselves with what others are doing. As Galatians tells us, we should take pride in what we are doing and not compare ourselves to others.

The Bible also teaches in 1 Corinthians 12 that God has uniquely gifted each of us. We each have our own talents to use. We are not like the other boys in the class or the co-workers down the hall. God has uniquely gifted us and expects us to use the gifts He has given us to our best ability and not worry about others.

As dads, we should help our boys discover the abilities God has given them. We should encourage them to try different things. We should encourage them to be open to new ideas. Many times we try to fit them into the box we fit into or the one we want them to fit into. We have to realize that their gifts come from God, not us. We must be careful not to hold our sons back because of our own fears and failures. God gives gifts to each one as He determines, not as we wish.

We must encourage and allow our boys to do what God has called them to and what they do best. It may not be the exact thing we would have picked for them, but we are not the ones living it. Of course they will learn and copy many things from us, but we should not force them to be just like us.

Allow your sons to be themselves and help them find who it is God wants them to be. It is better for us to help them find what it is God has for them than for them to go searching on their own in the world.

Get in the Game!

Here is your opportunity to make this eighth chapter real in your own life...

Do What You Do: *1 Samuel 17:38-4*

38 Then Saul dressed David in his own tunic. He put a coat of armor on him and a bronze helmet on his head. 39 David fastened on his sword over the tunic and tried walking around, because he was not used to them. "I cannot go in these," he said to Saul, "because I am not used to them." So he took them off. 40 Then he took his staff in his hand, chose five smooth stones from the stream, put them in the pouch of his shepherd's bag and, with his sling in his hand, approached the Philistine.

The Snap:

Boxes everywhere

"So he took them off"

Five smooth stones and a sling in his hand

The Pass:

Read Mark 3:21

Read Mark 6:3

Read Mark 8:27-29

What boxes did they try to put Jesus?

What did Jesus do?

John 13:1-8

What box do you put Jesus in?

Philippians 4:13, Ephesians 3:20

The Catch:

What will we choose?

Ephesians 6:13-17

Do what you do

Galatians 6:4-5

Chapter 9

Whose Team Are You On?

David said to the Philistine, "You come against me with sword and spear and javelin, but I come against you in the name of the LORD Almighty, the God of the armies of Israel, whom you have defied. This day the LORD will hand you over to me, and I'll strike you down and cut off your head. Today I will give the carcasses of the Philistine army to the birds of the air and the beasts of the earth, and the whole world will know that there is a God in Israel. All those gathered here will know that it is not by sword or spear that the LORD saves; for the battle is the LORD's, and he will give all of you into our hands" (1 Samuel 17:45-47).

DAVID'S HEART

At the end of verse 40, we read that David, "with sling in his hand, approached the Philistine." As in any good heavyweight bout, the two fighters began to size each other up. Both men – well, one man and one boy – came eye to eye. Verse 41 says Goliath kept coming closer to David, and from his response, he is both confused and insulted that the Israelites have sent a boy to fight him. Verse 42 says Goliath looked David over as if this were a joke.

Then the trash talking began. "Am I a dog that you come at me with sticks? Where is your sword little boy; that stick will not hurt me." Here was Goliath's first mistake, and one we sometimes make. He did not recognize the true danger. He saw a boy with a stick, but the reality was that it was a young man after God's own heart — who also happened to be an expert with the sling — who was coming at him.

The next mistake Goliath made was to insult the team David represented. The Bible says Goliath cursed David by his gods. It was one thing to underestimate the quality of his opponent, but a much greater mistake to underestimate the God of David. David was not your typical boy, and his God was not some worthless, pretend god. To Goliath, this was all about him against David. He was totally relying on his own ability to win. David, on the other hand, knew where his strength came from.

Growing up the youngest of eight brothers, David had probably heard his share of trash talk. He had probably even used a little himself. Can't you just see David running after that lion and bear telling them what he was going to do to them when he caught them?

This was a little different, however. This adversary talked back! This adversary began the trash talking. But David did not back down. He went right back at Goliath and told him what was really true.

Not the Players, But the Team

There is a saying in sports that sums up how to be successful: "It is not the team with the best players, but the players with the best team, that wins." We have all seen teams that are loaded with talent get whipped by teams with very little talent. The difference between the two teams is the word "team." One team is loaded with individuals; the other is loaded with members of a team. Goliath definitely had the most ability, but David had the best team.

After hearing Goliath put him and his team down, David stepped right up and told Goliath a thing or two. First, he acknowledged that Goliath was coming against him with only what he possessed physically, "a sword and spear and javelin." For Goliath it was all about what was with him; for David it was all about who was with him. He told Goliath that he had the "name of the Lord Almighty, the God of the Army of Israel." It was not about what David had, but who David had.

David knew that he was part of two teams that ensured his success. First, he was on the Lord Almighty's team. I am sure David had heard stories of the great things God had done for Abraham. He had heard about the Israelites amazing escape as Moses parted the Red Sea. He had heard of the great victories of Joshua and the Israelites. He knew his God was more than able to defeat the Philistines.

David knew there was a difference between the God of the Israelites and the so-called gods of the Philistines. He knew his God had real power while the gods of the Philistines had no power. There was a difference in the God he served and the false gods he was going up against. And history had proven his God the victor every time.

David also knew he was an Israelite. The name Israel literally means "to struggle with God." David had heard of the struggles his people had gone through: the time Abraham had to leave his homeland and go where God had called him. Then, Jacob was displaced to a Philistine land during a drought and God blessed him so that the Philistines forced him to leave. David had heard of the Israelite captivity in Egypt. He knew of the struggles his people had been through.

He also knew the difference between his people, the Israelites, and everyone else. It had nothing to do with the size or power of their army. It was certainly not about the amount of the land the Israelites possessed. No, it was all about the difference in the God they served.

The Israelites were God's chosen people. God had chosen to make Abram, later known as Abraham, into a great nation. He changed Abraham's son Jacob's name to Israel. It was their lineage that had been chosen. They had been set apart by God. David was from the lineage of Abraham, Isaac and Jacob. He knew who and where he had come from and he was proud of it.

What a heritage! It had to be powerful for David to know who and where he had come from. He knew what these great men had done and he knew greatness was in his blood. Look at the team he was on. It was the original dream team. This team had literally struggled with God. They had known great struggle, but had also known great victory.

David knew who his God was and the line of great men he belonged to. This combination gave him the confidence to tell Goliath, "Today I will give the carcasses of the Philistine army to the birds of the air." Now that's having confidence in your team!

For the Battle Is the Lord's

One thing David had learned from old stories was that when the Israelites trusted God, He delivered. He knew the common theme that when the Israelites submitted to God they had success, and when they relied on their own power they failed. David knew that as long as his God was doing the fighting, he would be just fine. This is why David told Goliath, "The battle is the Lord's."

David gave credit where credit was due (Romans 13:7) before he had even thrown a stone. He recognized he was not there in his own strength but in God's. He knew he could not win this fight without God's help. He also knew that God could not lose it. David told Goliath that God would give the Philistines into the Israelites' hands. Once again, this was not about David and Goliath, but about David's God against Goliath's gods. It was about God's chosen people. It was about the true God getting the glory.

This little battle between David and Goliath was about "the whole world knowing that there is a God in Israel." The message the Israelites had given for the past forty days was that they served a weak God. They had taken God out of the equation. And before that, the Israelites had rejected God by appointing a king and placing their faith in a man instead of God. David was putting God back at the center. He was placing the battle in God's hands. This was in stark contrast to what the rest of the Israelites were doing.

This is so much like our world today. We feel as if it is all about what we can do. We take God out of the equation. It is okay to go to church on Sundays, but God cannot go to the office with us on Mondays. We may go to a prayer group, but God is not with us when we are with our friends. We are like the rest of the Israelites; we only see our abilities when we face a Goliath. We do not even factor God into the fight.

David gives us such a different perspective, one only a man after God's own heart can give. If our hearts are like God's own heart, we will take God into every battle and place it into His hands. We will take Him in with us to see the boss that is so tough to get along with. We will take Him into our marriages and families and let Him save them. The God David takes into his battle is the same God who wants to fight our battles.

God wants to bless us so that He is glorified. David wants victory over Goliath so that the world would know that Israel has a God. God also wants to give us success, but it has nothing to do with us. It has everything to do with the whole world knowing who our God is. He wants the world to see how great He is through our actions and successes. He wants to bless us (though this is defined as His blessings, not just the perishable blessings we yearn for), but we have to be willing to let Him bless us.

We have to be willing to place the battle in God's hands. This is not easy. We want to have control. We want to make the decisions. We want to rely on worldly wisdom. However, God requires us to give everything to Him. He wants us to rely on His power. Are we willing to give our battles to the Lord? Are we willing to allow Him into our everyday lives? Are we willing to allow Him to take our careers where He wants them to go? Are we willing to give Him control of our families?

This is not what most self-help books recommend. However, it is what God requires. If we are to be men after God's own heart, we must be willing to place every battle in His hands. Whose team are we on?

JESUS' HEART

Isaiah 51:1 says, "Look at the rock from which you were cut and the quarry from which you were hewn." Isaiah is quoted many times in the New Testament, even by Jesus. I am sure Jesus knew and understood what Isaiah was saying in this verse. Jesus knew where He had come from and whose team He was on.

Matthew 1 gives us the genealogy of Jesus from Abraham to His earthly, adoptive father, Joseph. At that time, your genealogy was as important as anything. Where and from whom you came was very important. Jesus' lineage would give Him credibility among God's chosen people, for He was a descendent of Abraham, the father of the Jews.

Isaiah 11:1 goes on to say that the Messiah would come from the root of Jesse, and to prove this Old Testament prophesy was being fulfilled, Matthew showed Jesus was a direct descendant of David. Jesus' credentials matched His calling. He came from the correct family; He had the correct bloodline.

While Matthew gives us Jesus' earthly family, John gives us His spiritual family. He tells us in John 1:1-2 that Jesus had been with God from the beginning. This gives Jesus credibility when He claims to be the Son of God. Although He was fully human, He was also fully God. It was not enough just for Jesus to come from the right family, but in order to accomplish what He had come to do, He also had to be from God. This is such a hard concept to grasp, but it's worth grappling with. Jesus was not an ordinary man. Yes, He was fully human and experienced life just as we do, but He was and is also fully God, and this separates Him from us.

Like David, Jesus knew that what He was here for was much greater than Himself. It was not just about Jesus being in the world; it was about Him coming into the world to give people a chance to come to the Father. He represented not only an earthly family that had relied on God for all their success, but He also represented God. Similarly, David represented both the Israelites (his family) and the Lord Almighty to show the world that Israel had a God.

As John 1:8 points out about John the Baptist, "he himself was not the light: he came only as a witness to the light." Like David, Jesus was here to show the world the true light. This light was for every man. Jesus had not just come for the Jews; He had come for all of mankind. He had come to give others an opportunity to be a part of His family.

This was not about Jesus conquering death; it was about Jesus bringing the world to His Father. It was not about beating the giant, but showing the whole world that the one true God was Jesus' Father.

God's Team

Although it was of great importance that David and Jesus came from the right earthy families, it is of little importance who our earthly families are. God is not concerned with our genealogies. He is concerned about whether or not we know His Son. That is the most important team to God. The whole reason Jesus came was to allow everyone the opportunity to know His Father.

Galatians 3:26-29 gives a great insight into this key fact. We become sons of God through our faith in the fact that Jesus came to earth, lived a perfect life, died on the cross, and rose from the dead after three days. This is what God is more concerned about; it is the reason Jesus came to earth. God wants us to be on His team, or in His family, so badly that He sent His only Son to die for us so that we would be spared an eternal spiritual death.

Galatians 3:29 proclaims, "If you belong to Christ, then you are Abraham's seed, and heirs according to the promise." It is not about what earthly family we belong to, it is about whether or not we belong to Jesus. If we belong to Him, we are in God's family.

If we belong to Jesus, we can be sure that the same God who provided for Abraham will provide for us. The same God who parted the Red Sea will handle our road blocks. The same God who took Joshua into the promise land will be there for us in our battles. The same God who delivered Goliath into David's hands is the same God who goes before us when we face giants. The same God who raised Jesus from the dead is the same God who gives us eternal life. When we belong to Jesus, we belong to the same God who is over everything.

Ephesians 1:5 tells us that it gives God great pleasure to have us in His family. He longs to adopt us through Jesus. We can no longer make excuses about not being part of God's family. It has nothing to do with anyone but us. Humanly speaking, we make the decision whether to be part of His family.

Ephesians 3:6 tells us that it is a mystery, but that we are all part of the same family. No matter our ethnic background, our race, upbringing, failures, or talents. None of these things matter because we all share the same promise through Jesus, and that is eternal life. We are all part of the same family.

Whose family are you in? Whose team are you on?

LESSONS FROM JESSE

Do our boys know what we stand for? Do they know our past? Do they know where their family comes from? There is something about knowing our heritage. It is important to know the mistakes that have been made so we can keep from repeating them. It is great to know the sacrifices made so we can appreciate what we have. It is great to know our families' accomplishments so we can take courage from them. We have to share these memories and stories with our sons. They need to know and learn the good and bad from our past. This helps them to live in the future.

Families today often seem unconcerned about sharing their past. It is almost like we want our sons to write their own future. We want them to go out and conquer the world the way they want to. But this does not make much sense. Why would we not want them to learn from our mistakes so that they do not make the same ones? Why would we not want them to take courage from our accomplishments? Why would we not want them to know the sacrifices that have been made for them so they will learn to be grateful?

Deuteronomy 6:4-9 tells us to make sure we do not forget the commandments of God. Verse 7 says to "Impress them on our children." We are to talk about these things around the dinner table and when we walk down the street. We are to impart these things to our sons in everyday life. We should not rely on our sons learning these lessons at church, and definitely not at school. We must teach our sons about God's Word. We must teach them about right and wrong. We must teach our sons to love God. According to Deuteronomy 6, we should be doing this everywhere, all the time. It is *that* important.

I believe this is our most important role as fathers. We must make sure our boys know whose team they are on. I believe this is vital to raising men after God's own heart. If our boys do not know they are on God's team, then how can their hearts be like God's?

What Are We Telling Our Sons?

I can imagine David sitting around the camp fire listening to Jesse and his brothers telling stories. Jesse might be sitting back listening to his boys tell the stories he had told them in the past. I am sure they told the story about God providing a lamb for Abraham when he went to sacrifice Isaac. Then there was the time Joseph was sold into slavery. And who could forget the story of Moses and the burning bush? The stories would go on and on. And all of them had the same thing in common: the God of the Israelites came through again and again. Why would David not expect his God to deliver him from Goliath?

What are the stories our sons hear about God from us? Do they think they are made up or do they believe they serve the same God? We should be telling our boys certain types of stories. Stories of when God made Himself known. Stories of how great our God is and of the great things He has done. We should tell of the things God has done in our lives, no matter how big or small they may seem. Our sons need to know the God we serve is alive and well. They need to hear it from us.

One of the memories I have goes back to when I was in the eighth grade. My dad had just taken a coaching job in Albertville, Alabama, and we had moved there to join him. I do not know how long we had been there, or how many churches we visited, but I do remember when my family walked the aisle to join our church. My dad said something to the preacher that has stuck with me all these years. He told the pastor of the First Baptist Church that we were Christians first and Baptists second. I am not sure why, but things just clicked for me after hearing that statement.

We were Christians first. I remember being proud that he had used the pronoun "we." He had included me. I remember many times in my life thinking back to this statement and remembering that I am a Christian first. That statement really lets me know who I am. I had asked Jesus into my heart when I was seven years old, but my dad's statement had made that decision more clear to me. Now I knew that I was a Christian first. Before anything else, I put Jesus first. This would make future decisions much easier for me.

This statement also helped me understand my dad better. Now I understood why I never heard my dad use bad language. I understood why he wanted to do things right. I understood why my dad wanted me to be around the right people. I understood why he treated others the way he did. This one statement helped me understand many things about who my dad was and who I wanted to be. It was a simple statement that my dad made; one he perhaps did not realize the significance of at the time. He made the statement because that was who he was. He knew whose team he was on, and through him I knew whose team I was on. What do the statements we make say about what team we are on? Do our sons hear and see that we and they are on God's team?

115

We do not know which statements are going to impact our boys, but we do know our statements impact them. What our sons hear from us helps them understand not only who we are, but also who they will become. Our sons hear what we say to others. How will what we say impact them?

What Are You Showing Your Sons?

Not only are our boys listening to what we say, they are also watching what we do. They see every move we make. Don't think that David did not watch his father and older brothers to learn what to do. David saw his father's obedience to God and he saw how Jesse had instilled this into his older brothers. The Bible includes a few examples of this.

When Samuel came to anoint one of Jesse's sons as king, he first had to consecrate them before they could join him for the sacrifice (1 Samuel 16:5). I believe this was a great example of obedience for Jesse's boys to see. Jesse knew who his God was and knew he was unclean and unworthy to stand and worship God without being consecrated. This was a way of showing his boys that God came first.

Another example came when Jesse sent David to see his brothers during the battle. Do you remember the specific instructions he game David? One of the things he told David to do was to bring back some assurance from his brothers (1 Samuel 17:18). Jesse knew that if his sons had gained anything during this battle they needed to give back to God. He gave his boys another reason to know that God was first in his life and he was creating that attitude in them. He was making sure they did not think they were able to do anything in their own strength.

My dad was a high school football coach for forty years, and one of the joys of my life has been taking my two boys to his games. Dad was very successful and led one of the top programs in the state of Georgia. During his last season to coach, the boys (nine and six years old) and I jumped in the car every Friday night and made the four-hour drive to be on the sidelines for the game. It was a great year and the team played very well. The boys were able to be in the locker room, go through the run-through sign, be the water boys, run out and get the tee, ride the bus, and so many other things that are thrilling for any sports-driven boy.

One thing happened in the locker room before every game that I cherish more than anything. Each Friday night before my dad stood in front of the team to give them their last pep talk, he huddled up with a group of men (coaches) to pray to God and give Him the glory. His team was always important to him, but he still put being a Christian first. He wanted the whole world to know that Conrad Nix and the Northside High School football team have a God — just like David wanted the world to know that Israel had a God.

But that is not the best part. The best part was that my two boys got to join their dad, their granddad, and their uncle in that circle to praise God. The first time it happened I wept like a baby – I am weeping now as I write this – because I realized my boys were getting to see their dad in the same light I had seen my dad. I had grown up with my dad praying in locker rooms, and now my boys were seeing not only their dad but also their uncle and granddad do the same. What an example to see. What a legacy to leave. I think my boys know very clearly whose team we are on; as Joshua said, "As for me and my house we will serve the Lord."

"Impressing Them on Our Children"

My wife and I have seen the blessings of "impressing them on our children" this year. Not that I am saying we are great parents because, believe me, sometimes I wonder if our children will survive our parenting. But God has heard our prayers and has blessed us — or at least overcome our mistakes.

At nine years old, our son Bo had a school assignment to write a few things about himself. He put the usual: I love sports, I have two sisters and a brother, I love Auburn, and I have blond hair. The same kinds of things every third grader puts. But there was one thing he put that was extra special to mom and dad. There was a question about what made him unique and his answer was that he was a Christian.

I know this is not some monumental event, but for my boy to write that at school when I was not around makes me proud. Maybe somehow he has heard or seen from us that we are on God's team.

Another thing happened during our flag football season with our then six-year-old, Caleb. Each week before our games the other coach or I got the boys in a circle and lead a prayer. One week I asked if any of the boys wanted to lead the prayer. Caleb looked up and said, "I will." His prayer was not some prophetic prayer or anything, but just the fact that he was willing to pray made me proud. I could not help but think of the times he had stood in that circle with his dad, granddad, uncle, brother and other coaches. Praying before a game to give God glory was not something new for him. He had done this before. This exact thing had been modeled for him in the past. He knew he was on God's team and was not ashamed of it.

To go back to the original question: Whose team are we on? Whose team do our sons think we are on? What our sons hear us say, and what they see us do, lets them know whose team we and they are on. We must be careful what they are hearing and seeing from us. We must live Deuteronomy 6. We must tie God's Word on our hand like symbols and bind them on our foreheads for everyone to see. We must write them on our doorframes and on our gates. We must let our boys hear and see it from us in every area.

If we are on God's team, we must be on God's team all the time. Joshua 24:15 says, "Choose you this day whom you will serve, but as for me and my house, we will serve the Lord."

Get in the Game!

Here is your opportunity to make this ninth chapter real in your own life...

Whose team are you on? *1 Samuel 17:41-47*

41 Meanwhile, the Philistine, with his shield bearer in front of him, kept coming closer to David. 42 He looked David over and saw that he was only a boy, ruddy and handsome, and he despised him. 43 He said to David, "Am I a dog, that you come at me with sticks?" And the Philistine cursed David by his gods. 44 "Come here," he said, "and I'll give your flesh to the birds of the air and the beasts of the field!"

45 David said to the Philistine, "You come against me with sword and spear and javelin, but I come against you in the name of the LORD Almighty, the God of the armies of Israel, whom you have defied. 46 This day the LORD will hand you over to me, and I'll strike you down and cut off your head. Today I will give the carcasses of the Philistine army to the birds of the air and the beasts of the earth, and the whole world will know that there is a God in Israel. 47 All those gathered here will know that it is not by sword or spear that the LORD saves; for the battle is the LORD's, and he will give all of you into our hands."

The Snap:

Trash talk

Who were David's teams?

What were David's motives?

"For the battle is the Lord's" – not what, but who

The Pass:

What were Jesus' teams?

Matthew 1:1, John 1:1-2

What does Jesus do about the teams?

Galatians 3:26-29

The Catch:

What are our teams?

Ephesians 1:5, Ephesians 3:6

What does this verse mean for you and me?

"Listen to me, you who pursue righteousness and who seek the Lord: Look to the rock from which you were cut and to the quarry from which you were hewn" (Isaiah 51:1).

Chapter 10
Run Quickly Toward the Line

As the Philistine moved closer to attack him, David ran quickly toward the battle line to meet him. Reaching into his bag and taking out a stone, he slung it and struck the Philistine on the forehead. The stone sank into his forehead, and he fell facedown on the ground. So David triumphed over the Philistine with a sling and a stone; without a sword in his hand he struck down the Philistine and killed him (1 Samuel 17:48-50).

DAVID'S HEART

What a day it had been for David. It started out as a simple assignment from his dad and turned into an opportunity to glorify God. He could never have imagined standing in front of Goliath when he got up that morning. I am sure he never thought he would be using his sling in this way.

Consider everything David had been through just that day. He had gotten up first thing that morning and walked to the battle. Once there he got all excited when the war cries began and he knew it was time to go to battle. Then he was confused at how the Israelites reacted in fear toward Goliath.

If all this was not enough, he then had to deal with his older brother coming down on him harshly and the king telling him he was not big enough to fight Goliath. Once he got through this, he then had to deal with King Saul's efforts to outfit him as a warrior. Finally, after he was back in his own clothes and had his sling in his hand, he came face to face with a giant who was talking smack and who wanted to kill him.

Do we have any timeouts left? Now would be a good time to regroup and catch our breath, but not for David. He was ready for battle. He knew he was prepared for this and that the Lord Almighty was on his side. What more could he need? There was no time for a timeout; here came the giant!

Where Are You Running?

If David was going to run, now was the time. The Bible tells us "the Philistine was moving closer to attack him." This was David's last chance. Surely he would run. The Israelites on the hill looked down into the valley and they may have been thinking and possibly even saying, "Run David, run." After all, it was what they had done. Verse 24 notes that, "When the Israelites saw the man (Goliath), they all ran from him in great fear." *He will kill you David — run!*

Run is exactly what David did. Just not the way the other Israelites had already ran. Instead of running away from Goliath, verse 48 says, "David ran quickly toward the battle line to meet him." *Are you crazy, David? Go the other way!*

This is such an awesome verse. I just love the picture; this boy with a sling running toward this mighty man with his sword. Notice it does not say that David just approached the line. He had no hesitation, no second thoughts. He knew what he was going to do. "David ran quickly toward the line to meet him." Now that is a young man after God's own heart.

How many times are we faced with giants and we run from them in fear? We do not know how to handle them or we are scared of getting hurt. David could have been scared of getting killed. He did not have to fight the giant. That was not in his job description. However, this giant had defied the God of Israel and David was not going to sit around and let that happen.

Do we run quickly to the line to meet the giant or do we run in fear from him? We must make the decision as David did that we will run toward our giants and face them. We cannot run away from tough situations. When our marriages are struggling we must run quickly to the line to fight for them. When our sons need us, we must run quickly to the line to be there for them. When Jesus calls us to do something we must run quickly to the line to do it.

Where are we running? Are we running away from the giant or are we running toward him? It certainly is easier to run away, and as we saw with the rest of the Israelites, it is the most popular choice. True men after God's own heart do not choose the easiest or most popular way; they choose God's way. Where are you running?

Seems Awfully Lonely Out Here

Did you notice in verse 39 that King Saul and the rest of the Israelites seemed to disappear? It is almost as though they told David, "Hey man, I left something up on the hill, and I need to go get it." Then everyone disappeared and David was left alone. Even Goliath had a shield bearer with him. All David had was his staff, his sling, and five smooth stones. But that was all he needed.

Do you think David looked around and thought, "Hey, where did everybody go?" Or do you think he even noticed?

When we go to face our giants we may feel very lonely. This is not the most popular choice. The most popular choice is to let our marriages go. If half of marriages end in divorce anyway, why try to save ours? Why try to spend time with our sons when we can just buy them something instead? Why not hang out with the guys or stay at work a little longer? No need to read that Bible; we know we're going to make mistakes; we're just doing the best we can. Why should we stop drinking or doing drugs; it makes us feel so good, for a brief time anyway.

When we try to be a man after God's own heart, we will feel lonely at times. Not many people are willing to go down in the valley to take on the giant with us. It is too easy to stay on that hill and let someone else do it. We love to stay in our comfort zones. We can manage the danger in our comfort zones. We do not have to make those hard and unpopular decisions.

However, if we want to be men after God's own heart, we must come down into the valley to take on the giant, even if we have to go alone.

Who Are You Running To?

I believe the biggest question is whether David was running toward Goliath or toward God. I believe David was running toward God and Goliath just happened to be in the way. David had already declared that the battle was the Lord's. He was not running to fight Goliath; he was running to show the whole world that there was a God in Israel.

Jeremiah 9:23-24 says, "Let not the wise man boast of his wisdom or the strong man boast of his strength or the rich man boast of his riches, but let him who boasts boast in this: that he understands and knows me, that I am the Lord, who exercises kindness, justice and righteousness on earth, for in these I delight, declares the Lord."

These two verses sum up the difference between David and Goliath. Goliath came out for forty days and nights and boasted of his power and strength. It was all about Goliath.

In contrast, David came out and boasted in the name of the Lord Almighty, the God of the Israelites. David said it was not by sword or spear, but by the Lord that he would win. He boasted that he understood and knew God. He was not running to fight Goliath; he was running to show the world Israel had a God.

When we face giants in our lives we must be careful not to think it is by our strength or wisdom that we are able to stand, but it is through the power of Jesus Christ. Philippians 4:13 says we can do all things through Christ who gives us strength. It is not by our own works so no man can boast (Ephesians 2:9).

Psalm 147:10-11 says of the Lord, "His pleasure is not in the strength of the horse, nor his delight in the legs of a man: the Lord delights in those who fear him, who put their hope in his unfailing love."

We must learn this lesson from David and the Bible and know that if we take on the giant in our own strength, we will fail. We must rely on God's strength. We must boast in the fact that we understand and know God.

We must not run into the valley toward the giant, but run into the valley toward Jesus' unfailing love. And if a giant gets in the way, then kill him.

"Reaching into His Bag"

David went to face the giant for all the right reasons. He went to show the world who his God was. He was going fully prepared; he had killed a lion and a bear. He took with him what he knew he could use – his sling. But he still had to reach in his bag, take a stone and kill the giant with it. God could have killed Goliath without David lifting a finger, but David was prepared to do the work.

It should be the same with us. We cannot expect God to do everything for us. He will prepare us and give us all we need, but many times we still have to reach in our bags, take out a stone and kill the giant ourselves. God had provided David with everything he needed to defeat the giant, but David still had to do it.

It reminds me of the story of a man who refused to be saved during a flood. As the flooding began, a truck came by his house and he was told to get in and save himself. The old man said he did not need a ride; God would save him. Later, as the first floor of his house flooded, a boat came by to rescue him. Once again, the man said that God would save him. Finally, as the whole house was underwater, a helicopter came by to save him. But once again, the man said that God would save him. Well, after he died and found himself in front of Saint Peter, the man asked why God had not saved him. Peter replied, "Goodness, God sent a truck, a boat and a helicopter. What more could he do?"

We act the same way sometimes. We think that if we are good enough, somehow God will magically make our problems go away. Well, it seldom works that way. God can certainly do things without our help, but most things happen to us so we can exercise our God-given faith and abilities. God is trying to strengthen us through these trials. He provides us with talent and preparation to handle these situations. We must use what we have been given and take advantage of the preparation God has provided.

We must recognize the abilities God has given us and take advantage of the preparation He has put us through so we can reach into our bag when the time comes. We cannot go into the valley to take on the giant and expect God to do everything. He will provide all we need to kill the giant, but we still have to reach into our bag, take out a stone and sling it at the giant.

JESUS' HEART

Where Did Jesus Run?

Jesus spent three years performing miracles and teaching the people, but now the time had come for what He was really on earth to do. Jesus, like David, had to decide which direction to run. He had opportunity and reason to turn and run the other way, but instead He ran straight to meet the giant, which in His case would mean death.

We know from several verses that Jesus knew what He was about to go through. He understood how difficult it would be. In Matthew 26:38 Jesus tells His disciples, "My soul is overwhelmed with sorrow to the point of death." Luke 22:44 says that Jesus was in such anguish His sweat was like blood. Jesus prayed, "My Father, if it is possible, may this cup be taken from me." Jesus knew a brutal death awaited Him. Would He run to or away from the giant?

After Jesus finished praying in the garden, He told His disciples, "Rise, let us go! Here comes my betrayer!" But Jesus did not run away. He did not wait for His enemy to find Him. He approached them. Jesus went to his betrayer, ready to do battle.

The Greek word for "let us go" is *agwmen*. It means to lead, take with, or to take or bring to a destination (Net Bible). This gives us a much different view of this scene than we usually have. In a number of movies and stories about Jesus in the garden, He is standing behind His disciples. He is not necessarily hiding, but He is not out front. But the true interpretation is that Jesus actually led His disciples to meet His betrayer. Jesus was out front. He led His disciples to this encounter with His betrayer.

Once Jesus had awakened His disciples and led them to His betrayer, John 18:4 says, "Jesus, knowing all that was going to happen to him, went out and asked them, 'Who is it you want?'" This verse confirms all that we have been looking at. Jesus knew what was in store for Him. He knew He would be arrested, beaten and even crucified. He knew this was not going to be easy. But, even knowing all this, He still "went out and asked."

I believe Jesus did this to make sure His Father's will was done. What if Judas chickened out? What if the soldiers said they could not find Him? Jesus knew what had to be done. He knew it was time. He made sure His Father's will was carried out. He took no chances. He went out to meet them. Jesus went out and asked who they were looking for. Like David, He ran quickly to the line to meet them.

Where Did Everybody Go?

It can be very lonely when we are in God's will. As we saw with David, Jesus also ended up alone when he went to face the giant. It started for Jesus when He took His disciples, the men He knew He could count on, with Him to the garden to pray. Then He took Peter, James and John, His three closest disciples, farther into the garden with Him. This would be a pretty good group to take to a prayer meeting. This was not a bunch of rejects; these guys were the real deal. There was no way they would abandon Jesus.

However, once they got into the garden, even the disciples abandoned Jesus. He went away three separate times to pray by Himself, telling the disciples to pray for Him. All three times Jesus returned and found them sleeping. Jesus asked them in Matthew 26:40, "Could you men not keep watch with me for one hour?" Jesus was all alone when He went to pray. He longed for His disciples to pray with and for Him, but He found Himself all alone. Many times we will find ourselves alone in prayer. We will want others to join us, but when we look around it will just be us. This did not stop Jesus from praying and it should not stop us from praying.

After Jesus was arrested He once again finds Himself alone. Mark 14:27 quotes Zechariah 13:7, "I will strike the shepherd, and the sheep will be scattered." That is exactly what happened when Jesus was arrested. The sheep scattered without their shepherd. Mark 14:50 says, "Then everyone deserted him and fled."

We have all had this feeling. The feeling that we are all alone; that it is us versus the world. Most of the time our spouse or parents are still there for us. Or maybe our closest friends might not agree with us, but they usually do not desert us. But sometimes we are just all by ourselves. Our closest friends and family have fled. Does this mean we give up? Do we stay on the hill with the rest of the Israelites?

I believe it means that we must be sure we are in God's will, and if we are, then by all means we must run quickly to the line! We should realize that when we run quickly to the line we will leave most others behind us. It takes courage to run forward. It takes great faith in our team and in Jesus Christ. We must know that we are fighting the battle God wants us to fight. If we are, then even if we are alone we must fight anyway.

Jesus had already predicted that He would be deserted. We too can know that when we are in the will of God, there will be times when we will be deserted. Sometimes it is lonely when we are doing God's will, but do it we must if we want to be men after God's own heart.

What Was Jesus Running To?

It is more important to understand what Jesus was running to than exactly where he was running. Anyone can blindly run into danger and try to be a martyr. But we must be sure that if we are going to run into a battle, it is a battle worth fighting. We saw that David was not running to fight Goliath as much as he was running quickly to the line to show the world that there was a God in Israel. David was running to God and Goliath just happened to be the way. Jesus did the same thing.

Jesus knew where He was running and why He was running there. If He wanted to be an earthly king then He was running in the wrong direction. Jesus knew that this was His Father's will and that it was God's plan for His life. In Mark 14:36 Jesus says, "Yet not my will but yours be done." It was not about Jesus, it was about God's will. It was not an easy path for Jesus, but it was the only way to conquer death.

In Matthew 17:22-23 Jesus predicted what would happen to Him. He knew He would be betrayed, arrested, crucified and raised on the third day. He knew He was running to the cross when He ran quickly to meet His betrayer. Jesus was not running just to die; He was running to save the world. I am so glad He decided to tell His disciples to get up and follow Him to meet His betrayer.

Jesus lived out Jeremiah 9:23-24; He did not boast in His strength, knowledge or riches. Jesus boasted in the fact that He knew His Father and understood His Father's will. He did not go to the cross for His own good; He went for His Father's glory. Are we running to the line for the glory of God? Do we run quickly to the line to show the world that our God is real? What do we boast about? Ephesians 2:8-9 says, "for it is by grace you have been saved, through faith — and this not from yourselves, it is the gift of God — not by works, so that no man can boast."

If we are going to run to the line, we should make sure we are running to glorify God and not for our own benefit. Victory will only come through Jesus Christ.

LESSONS FROM JESSE

Jesse Ran Too

We all want our sons to be the ones to take on giants. The ones who stand up against injustice. The ones who protect those who have been wronged. We want our boys to be the ones the world can count on to do what is right. We want our boys to be the ones who are willing to run quickly to the line to meet the opposition. We want all these things, but what are we doing to see that our boys are willing to do them? Are we teaching them to run to or away from giants?

David and Jesus had a choice in the direction they would run. Logic and reasoning told them to turn and run the other way. The world certainly did not expect them to run toward the giant. But both of them chose to run right into the heart of trouble. They did not back down from what they knew God wanted them to do. Where did they learn this? Where did their motivation come from?

I believe we can look at their dads and see where their role models came from. Jesse had to make the choice of which direction he would run long before David would make his choice. When God told Samuel to go to Jesse to pick one of his sons to be the next king, Samuel feared for his life. In 1 Samuel 16:2, Samuel replied to God, "How can I go? Saul will hear about it and kill me." It seems likely that if Samuel feared for his life, Jesse would have the same fear. Jesse was choosing to run in the direction of danger when he chose to listen to Samuel.

Also, we read that when Samuel "arrived in Bethlehem, the elders of the town trembled when they met him" (1 Samuel 16:4). During the time of Samuel, whenever he came to the people it was usually to tell them how wicked they were and how God was going to punish them. The people had every right to tremble when Samuel came to town. Jesse had every right to tremble when Samuel came to him. Jesse would have to choose whether he would run away from Samuel or toward him.

What would Jesse do? Would he run and hide in fear of King Saul? Would he run because he feared what Samuel had to say to him? No, Jesse would not run from Samuel in fear, although he had every reason to. He would meet Samuel and do what the prophet asked. He did not question what Samuel was doing or try to avoid the situation. It is no wonder David "ran quickly to the line to meet Goliath." That is the lesson his dad had modeled for him.

We live in a time that is very similar to when Jesse lived. Our society has also forsaken our God in so many areas and has decided to take on other kings than God. We too have many reasons to fear and run when it comes time to do what God wants us to do. But is this the example we want our boys to see? They need to see us running quickly to the battle line, not running away from it. This is not the easy and popular choice, and it may even cost us something, but it is the direction we must run.

Our boys must see us run toward the battle line, not away. David saw his dad run to battle and our boys need to see the same thing from us.

Which way are you running?

What Are You Running To?

Even more important than the fact that Jesse ran toward the battle line is the fact that he ran to meet his God. I pointed out that David was running more toward his God than Goliath, and I believe we see the same thing with Jesse when Samuel came calling. Jesse did not know the reason for Samuel's visit, but he did know Samuel was a prophet of God and he wanted to run toward that.

It took time and effort for Samuel to prepare Jesse and his sons to come before the Lord. Samuel consecrated Jesse and his sons and invited them to the sacrifice. I imagine this had to excite Jesse. He had the opportunity to come before the Lord with Samuel. Jesse ran to get this chance. He ran to come before the Lord, not to meet with Samuel.

Do our boys see us run to be before the Lord, or do they see us run to get in front of the television? Do our boys see us run to get before the Lord or do they see us run out the door to work? I believe David saw his dad run toward the Lord and because of this example he knew which direction to run. Our boys are going to run in the direction we teach them to run. More important, our boys are going to run to the same things they see us run to.

Giants Along the Way

As we saw with David, when we run toward God we will encounter giants along the way. But if we keep our focus on our Lord we will be able to slay them. I am sure it was not easy for Jesse to accept the fact that his youngest son was selected as the next king. It had to be tough dealing with the rest of his sons and the emotions they went through seeing their younger brother chosen instead of them. I am sure it was tough dealing with his countrymen as word spread of David. No one said running toward the Lord would be easy and Jesse would have to face the giants as they came. But he would continue to run toward the Lord as he faced those giants.

We must prepare our boys for the same challenges. Our boys must know that when they run toward Jesus they will face giants along the way. We must teach and show our boys through example that as long as we continue to run toward Jesus, He will give us all we need to defeat the giants in our lives. David had seen Jesse deal with tough situations as he was growing up. I have to believe that he also saw his dad continue to focus on and run toward the Lord. When it came time for David to face his giant, he knew to focus on the Lord and keep running to Him.

Are our boys seeing the same thing? Who do we run to when times get tough? Do we run to the bottle when we face a giant? Do we run to seclusion when we face a giant? Or do our boys see us reach into our bag and take out a stone and keep running to our Lord?

We will face giants in our lives and how we react to them will be how our boys react to the giants in their lives. I hope we as dads will learn from Jesse and continue to focus and run toward our Lord during these times.

Get in the Game!

Here is your opportunity to make Chapter 10 real in your own life...

Run Quickly to the Line: *1 Samuel 17:48-50*

48 As the Philistine moved closer to attack him, David ran quickly toward the battle line to meet him. 49 Reaching into his bag and taking out a stone, he slung it and struck the Philistine on the forehead. The stone sank into his forehead, and he fell facedown on the ground.

The Snap:

Where and how was David running?

Where did everybody go?

Who was David running to?

Psalm 147:10-11

Reaching into his bag

1 Corinthians 10:13

The Pass:

Read Matthew 26:46 — agwmen

Read John 18:4

Read Mark 14:50

Where did Jesus run?

What did Jesus run to?

Where did everybody go?

The Catch

Jeremiah 9:23-24 — where do you run?

Romans 8:31 & 37 — reach into your bag

Now *agwmen*!

Chapter 11
Finish the Job

So David triumphed over the Philistine with a sling and a stone; without a sword in his hand he struck down the Philistine and killed him.

David ran and stood over him. He took hold of the Philistine's sword and drew it from the sheath. After he killed him, he cut off his head with the sword.

When the Philistines saw that their hero was dead, they turned and ran. Then the men of Israel and Judah surged forward with a shout and pursued the Philistines to the entrance of Gath and to the gates of Ekron. Their dead were strewn along the Shaaraim road to Gath and Ekron. When the Israelites returned from chasing the Philistines, they plundered their camp.

David took the Philistine's head and brought it to Jerusalem; he put the Philistine's weapons in his own tent.

As soon as David returned from killing the Philistine, Abner took him and brought him before Saul, with David still holding the Philistine's head (1 Samuel 17:50-54, 57).

DAVID'S HEART

The United States hockey team's victory over the Russian team in the 1980 Winter Olympics is known as one of the greatest upsets in sports history. It featured a U.S. team made up of a group of college kids who only became a team in 1979 facing off against a Russian team that had won four straight Winter Olympic Hockey gold medals. It was very unlikely the U.S. team would even advance to have a chance to play the Russians, much less beat them.

As unlikely as it seemed, the United States team found a way to advance to the medal round to play the Russians. These were the same teams that just weeks earlier had played an exhibition game in which the Russians dominated in a 10-3 victory. But on February 22, 1980, the impossible happened. Something that had not occurred since 1960 would happen; the Russians would not win gold. In a stunning 4-3 victory, the U.S. defeated the invincible Russians.

Most people believe this victory gave the United States the gold medal, but it did not. The U.S. team still had to win one more game to earn gold. They had done the impossible by beating the Russians, but they had to finish the job in order to receive gold medals. Two days after defeating the Russians the U.S. beat Finland 4-2 to win gold in the 1980 Winter Olympics.

The win over the Russians is what people remember, but it was actually finishing off the Finns that gave the U.S. the gold. It makes you wonder if the great victory over the Russians would have been tainted in any way had they lost to Finland. Had the U.S. not finished on top, what would their legacy be? We will never know because they finished the job they came to do. Yes, beating the Russians was a huge upset, but they had to finish well in order to win the gold.

David faced this same kind of challenge. He dropped Goliath with one stone, but the battle was not over. The impossible had happened—the giant had been defeated—but there was still more to do. David had to finish the job in order for the Israelites to win the battle.

Don't Celebrate Too Soon

How many times in sports have we seen one team score near the end of a game and start celebrating, thinking they have won, only to have the other team come back and score, stealing the victory away from them? We have to be careful about celebrating too early. David had every reason to celebrate after he hit Goliath in the forehead. But once again he showed great wisdom and discipline. Instead of celebrating this victory prematurely, he finished the job.

Most of us would be doing a victory dance if we were David. He had just done what no one thought he could. He could have let his guard down and boasted in his victory, but as we will see later, he had to finish off Goliath to finish off the battle.

I believe it is during these times of victory in our lives that we are most vulnerable. It is during these times that we relax and think we have nothing to worry about. Satan is just waiting for us to relax, to let our guard down so he can attack (1 Corinthians 10:12). It is during these times after a great victory that we can allow Satan to get a foot in the door. We take our eyes off of our mission and off of God and look at our accomplishments. If we believe for a second that it is about us, Satan will use this pride to bring us down.

David did not allow pride to overcome him. He kept his focus on his mission. He kept his focus on the fact that "the battle is the Lord's." He finished what he started. He did not allow the Philistines to get away. The battle was not about David versus Goliath; it was about the Israelites, God's chosen people, against the Philistines. We must also remember it is not about us winning a victory, but it is about us living for God. If we live for God on earth every day, the real celebration will come when we stand before Him in heaven.

Did David Have to Be so Extreme?

It seems a bit extreme for David to stand over Goliath, take the giant's own sword and cut off his head. Did he have to be so extreme? Today we consider his actions a little over the top. Similarly, Christians are sometimes labeled as extremist because they are over the top about obeying God. People wonder "Do they have to be so judgmental? How come they are so narrow minded?"

In David's case, the Bible is pretty clear that cutting off Goliath's head was needed and the act played a major role in the Israelites' subsequent victory. David was down in the valley with Goliath and no one had come with him. Everyone else was on the hill; the Philistines on one side of the valley and the Israelites on the other. They were looking down on the fight between David and Goliath from a safe distance.

As they saw Goliath get struck on the forehead and go down, they may have wondered if he was dead or not. Did the stone just knock him out? Is Goliath going to get up? David made it very clear Goliath was not getting up when he went over and cut off Goliath's head with his own sword. The Philistine champion had been killed and there was no doubt about it.

The Philistines did not know if Goliath was dead until David cut off his head. The end of verse 51 says, "When the Philistines saw that their hero was dead, they turned and ran." Once they realized their champion was dead, they ran for their lives.

Neither did the Israelites respond until after David cut off Goliath's head. I am sure they were standing on the hill in disbelief when they saw Goliath fall to the ground and were also unsure of what to do. But as soon as they saw David with Goliath's head, verse 52 says they "surged forward with a shout and pursued the Philistines." The Israelites may have stayed on the hill all day if David had not cut off Goliath's head. But this act energized them and they pursued their enemies with confidence.

Killing Goliath was not enough. David had to finish the job and go to the extreme of cutting off the giant's head for the Israelites to win the battle. No one moved on either hill until he had finished off Goliath. David had to be extreme for both the Israelites and the Philistines to see what the Lord had done. Many times we face a similar situation. People are standing on the hill looking at us in the valley, waiting to see how we respond. They watch to see if we celebrate by taking credit ourselves or if we are extreme and continue to focus on Jesus. There are times when the world may view us as being extreme, but at least they know where we stand. Do the people around us know whose team we are on? Are we viewed as being extreme sometimes?

Being a whole-hearted Bible-believing Christian can seem extreme in the eyes of the world, but the Bible gives many examples of people who were extreme in how they followed the Lord. Abraham was extreme when he placed Isaac on the altar to be sacrificed. Moses was extreme when he led the Israelites through the Red Sea on dry ground. Daniel was extreme when he refused to stop praying and was thrown into the lion's den. Shadrach, Meshach, and Abednego were extreme when they refused to bow to the idol

King Nebuchadnezzar had made and were thrown into the fiery furnace. Stephen was extreme when he chastised the Sanhedrin for "resisting the Holy Spirit" and was stoned as a result. Paul was extreme when he returned to the same city where he had just been stoned and left for dead because he was preaching the good news of Jesus Christ.

We cannot worry about what the world thinks of us; we can only worry about what God has called us to do. Romans 12:1 says, "...I urge you...in view of God's mercy, to offer your bodies as a living sacrifice, holy and pleasing to God." Now that sounds extreme. We are to offer ourselves to God, everything about us, everything we do. Not just when it is comfortable or when it seems right to the world. It is God's standard we are to live by, not society's standards or our own.

Romans 12:2 acknowledges that the world does not have the blueprint for living a life "holy and pleasing to God." It says, "Do not conform anymore to the pattern of this world, but be transformed by the renewing of your mind." The Bible warns us that the world will look at us as being different, maybe even extreme. That is why we must transform our minds and stay focused on God. This is the path to knowing "what God's will is – his good, pleasing and perfect will."

Being a sold-out believer is not easy, and never has been, but it has always been what God has called his people to be. We are to be totally dependent on God and that is extreme. Are we willing to be extreme? Are we willing to offer our bodies as living sacrifices to God? Are we willing to transform our minds? In order to live like this, sometimes we have to be extreme and figuratively cut off the head of the giant.

Still Holding the Philistine's Head

Do you remember the WWJD bracelets that were so popular years ago? You could not find a youth group anywhere whose kids were not wearing them. The bracelet was to be a constant reminder of the question, What Would Jesus Do? It was to be a constant reminder that in everything we did as Christians we were to be imitators of Jesus. There are many times in life when we need this reminder. In good times and bad, we have a tendency to take our eyes off Jesus and look at our problems or successes. We focus on ourselves instead of Jesus. We need constant reminders to keep our eyes focused on Him.

I believe that was why David still had the Philistine's head in his hand at the end of the battle. He had carried this grisly trophy around as a reminder. Seems pretty gross to me, but it would definitely be a constant reminder to David of what God had done; a reminder that the battle had been won but still had to be fought to the end. And a reminder to the Israelites and the Philistines of whom the one true God was.

We also need constant reminders of what God has done in our lives. We can look at times in our past and have confidence about our future. We can know that God has been there with us before and He will be there with us in the future. There are heads from our past that we need to carry around to remind ourselves that in good times and bad God has and will conquer all. Psalm 143:5 says, "I remember the days of long ago; I meditate on all your works and consider what your hands have done." We too should meditate on all the works God has done in our lives and let them serve as constant reminders.

David also carried the head as a reminder to the people, both the Israelites and the Philistines, that the victory had already been won. We are also in a battle—a spiritual battle—that has already been won, but just like the Israelites we must still fight. After David cut off Goliath's head, the Israelites knew the battle was over, but they still had to wipe out the Philistines. And we know that when Jesus came out of the tomb, the victory had been won, but we still have to battle Satan every day until Jesus returns. We can carry the cross with us as David carried the Philistine's head. We can know victory is ours; it is just a matter of time. But until then, we must continue to fight.

We may be going through tough times now and need a reminder of what God has done in our past. Times of struggle that He carried us through, or times of great success He blessed us with. No matter what the situation, we can do as the Psalmist says and remember the days long ago and meditate on the great things God has done in our lives. When we do this we too will show the world around us the one true God.

Just like David, Jesus had been preparing His whole life for the one moment to finish the job God had given Him. Once and for all He had the opportunity to conquer death. Jesus had spent three years in ministry preparing for this moment and now it was here. How would He finish the job?

Jesus took His stone and hit Satan right between the eyes when He hung on the cross. But as with David, no one was sure what had happened. As Jesus hung on the cross He uttered the famous words, "It is finished." But what did Jesus mean? Was He really finished? Was the fight over? No, Jesus was referring to the sin debt having been "paid in full." He was the ultimate sacrifice to forgive sin. No more would people have to offer sacrifices for the forgiveness of sin. No more would mankind be eternally separated from God. Jesus had paid the debt in full through His death.

His death, however, only confused people even more. Just as the Philistines and Israelites stood on the hill wondering if the giant was dead, people watched Jesus die and wondered if that was it. Both Jesus' followers and those who opposed Him had to wonder, is that it? They would receive their answer soon enough, but there was a great deal of confusion at first.

After Jesus was arrested, Mark 14:50 says, "Then everyone deserted him and fled." Even His closest friends did not know what to think. "Was this it?" they might have wondered. Had they followed Jesus, and given everything they had, for it to end like this?

Jesus Went to the Extreme

As we saw with David and many of the other patriarchs, sometimes obeying God can lead to extremes. Well, it does not get any more extreme than what Jesus did. Jesus died on a cross for people who were sinners—that would be me and you. That is extreme! We would have a hard time giving our lives for our families; there is no way we would die for wicked people who did not even love or care for us.

Jesus dying on the cross was only a part of God's plan. The rest of it was even more extreme. No wonder Jesus' disciples could not understand it. Not only did Jesus die for sinners, but He also rose from the dead.

Come on Jesus; do you have to be so extreme?

Matthew 28 reports that when the two Marys went to the tomb to see Jesus they found it empty. Once again to be a little more extreme, God sent an angel to announce, "He is not here: he has risen, just as he said." Afraid, the women hurried away to find the disciples.

Surely this whole salvation thing could have been done in a more believable way. Maybe that is why the Bible says in Matthew 7:14, "But small is the gate and narrow is the road that leads to life, and only a few find it."

This death and resurrection stuff is too extreme for some people. But as we saw with David, sometimes following God is extreme. Are we willing to believe this extreme story? Are we willing to let it change our lives?

Walking with Jesus

After David cut off Goliath's head, he carried it around with him as a reminder to himself and to everyone else. And concerning Jesus, Acts 1:3 tells us, "After his suffering, he showed himself to these men and gave many convincing proofs that he was alive. He appeared to them over a period of forty days and spoke about the kingdom of God." Jesus spent time with His disciples after His resurrection to give them something to remember. He gave them the proof they would need to change the world.

It had to be difficult for the disciples after Jesus' death. They had devoted their lives to following Him and now He was dead. Jesus knew how difficult this was for them. He also knew how important these men would be in finishing the job God had sent Him to do. Jesus had to give them something to carry with them so they would personally believe, as well as something they could give to others. Just as David carried the Philistines' head, the disciples would carry the words of Jesus and the fact that they had walked with Him after His resurrection.

We read over and over in the New Testament of the sufferings and persecutions the disciples faced. Life was a constant struggle and battle for them. They were persecuted on all sides. Being able to remember times of walking with Jesus provided strength that enabled them to continue. They carried the memory of Jesus with them to remind them of why they were doing what they were doing. Jesus knew how difficult it would be for them, but He also knew they would be able to succeed if they were able to remember walking with Him. They did not have to rely on their own strength or something they made up; they could walk in the truth of Jesus' resurrection.

Not only did the memory of walking with Jesus provide strength for them to carry His message, it was the message itself. Without walking with Jesus after His resurrection they would not have a story to tell. Because they had walked with Jesus, this was not a fairy tale they told but something real and true. They did not have to make up a story; they were able to tell what they had seen and heard. Acts 1:3 tells us Jesus had given them many convincing proofs to carry with them. He provided them with exactly what they needed to finish the job.

Do we have the memory of walking with Jesus to carry with us? If we do, then we can go in confidence with this memory. We need to carry this memory to give us strength and we need to share this story with others. If we do not have a memory of walking with Jesus, we need to pray God will give us this opportunity or shed light on the times we were walking with Him. Jesus wants to walk with us, and give us convincing proofs that He is alive, so we can personally have confidence and share this story with others.

Final Victory

Although David and the Israelites defeated the Philistines after he cut off Goliath's head, there would still be more battles to come. And we still have ongoing battles to face today. But there is a time coming when there will be no more battles. A time when final victory will be achieved and Jesus Christ will reign forever. Philippians 2 tells us that one day every knee will bow and every tongue will confess that Jesus Christ is Lord.

Revelation 19 and 20 give us a description of what the final battle will look like. Heaven will open up and Jesus will come down with the armies of heaven and declare war against the beast and all the evil of the world. The

Bible tells us, "then death and Hades will be thrown into the lake of fire." The battle will be over. There will be no more fighting; the Lord will have the victory! Jesus will have finished the job!

LESSONS FROM JESSE

In 1 Samuel 16 we can see where David may have learned how to finish from watching Jesse and Samuel. Jesse was a great example of not celebrating too early, being extreme in following God, and giving David something to remember. Of course Jesse had a great deal of help from Samuel, but Jesse still had to be willing to work with Samuel.

I can imagine that Jesse had mixed emotions when Samuel came to him. It had to be exciting for a man of God to come and invite you and your sons to join him in a very sacred ceremony. This was very special and not everyone had this opportunity. Jesse's chest had to swell a little. Of all the people Samuel could have chosen, he picked Jesse and his sons to join him. We do not see any pride from Jesse. We do not see him begin to celebrate. Instead he continues to do what Samuel asks of him.

This was not an obvious or easy process. The Bible tells us that Samuel thought the new king would be Jesse's firstborn, Eliab, when he saw him. But it was not Jesse's firstborn who would be chosen. Nor was it one of his next six sons. Neither Jesse nor Samuel had stopped to celebrate with the firstborn; they were waiting for the Lord to give them direction. They did not lose focus on God and use their own understanding. Maybe this is where David learned to keep his focus on God and not on his achievements. Do we stop short to celebrate or do we keep our focus on God to finish the job?

Jesse and Samuel were also extreme in their methods. After the first seven of Jesse's sons had been presented to Samuel, the Lord had still not chosen one of them to anoint as the next king. Samuel asked if these were all of his sons and Jesse admitted that his youngest was out tending the sheep. Samuel had Jesse send for David and insisted they would not sit down or change their course until he arrived. He was willing to be extreme and not lose focus until David came.

Now there had to be some time that passed before David showed up. It was not like they had cell phones to give David a call. They had to send someone to find him and bring him back. Samuel and Jesse were willing to be extreme and wait on David for as long as it took. They refused to turn their attention to anything else until they had done the work God had given them. David could have learned from this situation that sometimes you have to do extreme things to follow God. Maybe by the time David arrived they had been waiting for a long while and he could tell they were tired.

Maybe David thought this was not really extreme: it was just what you did when you followed God. Do our sons see following Jesus at all costs as something extreme or just something normal because it is what we have shown them? I think David just thought it was being normal because he had been given that example from his dad. It was only extreme to the rest of the world.

After Jesse presented David to Samuel, David was given something he could remember and carry with him. Firsts Samuel 16:13 says that David was anointed in the presence of his brothers and from that day the Spirit of the Lord was with him. David had an experience with God he could carry with him and his dad's obedience had a great deal to do with it. Jesse was willing to hold off celebrating and was willing to be extreme and wait for God. This patience, obedience and persistence enabled David to be anointed and have the power of the Spirit of the Lord with him.

What are we doing for our sons' salvation and for them to be filled with the Holy Spirit? As Jesse demonstrated, the best thing we can do is be obedient to God ourselves and to know that this will guide us with our sons.

I See Jesus Standing

The real finish in life is found in Revelation when everyone, great and small, stands before the throne of God. Revelation 20 tells us that books will be opened to judge the dead. One book will be used to determine who goes to heaven and who goes to hell. This is the Book of Life. The other book will be used to judge what we have done on earth. I believe the Bible teaches that we will all stand in front of this judgment seat and that one of three things will happen to us.

First, and worst of all, there will be many who stand before the judgment throne and, as Matthew 7 says, will cry "Lord, Lord," but God will "tell them plainly 'I never knew you. Away from me, you evil doers.'" These are people whose names are not in the Book of Life. There will be no need to judge what they have done because no matter what they have done, good or bad, they will be thrown into the lake of fire, which is the second death mentioned in Revelation 20:14. These people never called on Jesus to take the death penalty for their sins; therefore they must pay for their sins themselves. Romans 6:23 says, "For the wages of sin is death." If we do not allow Jesus to pay our death penalty, then we must pay it ourselves.

The second option is to stand in front of God and be allowed into heaven because our names are in the Book of Life. But when the other book is opened and we are judged, God will be disappointed to see what little we have done with our lives. First Corinthians 3:15 says that what we have done will be burned up, but we will be saved only as one escaping through the flames. Although such people will make it into heaven, they will not have anything to show for the lives they lived. They will not receive the reward they could have. Jesus will sit next to His Father and say, "Yes, I knew them, but they did nothing with their lives."

The last reaction – and the one we should all strive for – can be found in Acts 7:56. This is my life verse. It is how I want to finish my life. The setting is when Stephen is being stoned to death for chastising the Sanhedrin. As Stephen is about to die, he says, "Look, I see heaven open and the Son of Man standing at the right hand of God." Did you get that? Stephen saw Jesus standing at the right hand of God. Not sitting but standing! That sends chills down my spine. I just love that! Does that not get you excited? It is great motivation for me.

I can imagine Stephen getting to heaven and Jesus running to him to give him a high five. I can see Stephen and Jesus chest bumping. Now that is the kind of greeting I want to get in heaven. I want to live a life worthy of Jesus standing for me. I want to receive the reward that 1 Corinthians 3:14 talks about. I also want my boys to live lives worthy of Jesus standing for them.

We all want this for ourselves and our boys, but are we willing to live like it? Are we willing to do all the little things to help us finish our lives the way we should? Are we willing to be men after God's own heart? Are we willing to run quickly to the line to face the giant?

It takes a great deal of obedience and sacrifice to receive this reward. But the Bible is clear that this is to be our goal. We are to live lives that will cause Jesus to stand and greet us. It is definitely worth taking on the giant to receive this reward.

I hope and pray you will choose to live a life worthy of making Jesus Christ gladly stand!

Get in the Game!

Here is your opportunity to make this last chapter real in your own life...

Finish the Job: *1 Samuel 17:50-54, 57*

50 That's how David beat the Philistine—with a sling and a stone. He hit him and killed him. No sword for David!

51 Then David ran up to the Philistine and stood over him, pulled the giant's sword from its sheath, and finished the job by cutting off his head. When the Philistines saw that their great champion was dead, they scattered, running for their lives.

52-54 The men of Israel and Judah were up on their feet, shouting! They chased the Philistines all the way to the outskirts of Gath and the gates of Ekron. Wounded Philistines were strewn along the Shaaraim road all the way to Gath and Ekron. After chasing the Philistines, the Israelites came back and looted their camp. David took the Philistine's head and brought it to Jerusalem. But the giant's weapons he placed in his own tent.

57 As soon as David returned from killing the Philistine, Abner brought him, the Philistine's head still in his hand, straight to Saul. (The Message)

The Snap:

Why we are fighting?

Wasn't killing Goliath enough? Did David have to be so extreme?

What was the reaction to David's cutting off Goliath's head?

The Pass:

How did Jesus finish?

John 19:30

John 17:4-5

Matthew 28:6

Did all of this have to be so extreme?

The Catch:

Read Revelation 20:14b

Read Acts 7:56

How will Jesus react to you?

Acknowledgments

My thanks to...

...my mom and dad, Conrad and Patsy Nix. Thanks, Dad, for choosing for both you and your house to serve the Lord. Mom, thanks for always encouraging and believing in me. Thank you both for believing in this book.

...my in-laws, Jim and Lynda Sattler, for being such a godly example for my family.

...my father-in-law, the late Bob Chapman, for his love, support, and advice for Krista and for me during our young married life.

...David Sanford for his encouragement and work to make this book a reality. Thank you to Mike Hamel and Elizabeth Honeycutt for their editorial work. And thanks to Allison Williams for the cover photograph, to Anneli Anderson for the cover design, and to Erika Fitzpatrick for the interior design.

...John Hardie for the biblical foundation you helped establish in me during my college years.

...Bill Gray, Steve Hancock, Kevin Inman, and Derrick Moore for your friendship and accountability.

...the Davis boys (Jon, JD, Josh, and Jachin), the Lott boys (Ken, Travis and Nick) and the Price boys (Jeff, Drew, Jackson and Hunley) for your commitment to our Saturday morning Bible study.

... all the coaches out there; keep fighting the good fight. You are the only dad some of these players will ever have.

About the Author

Patrick Nix has loved the game of football all his life, but his real passion is his love for Jesus Christ. His faith journey began early as he witnessed the strong faith and biblical example of his own father and football coach, Coach Conrad Nix. More importantly than teaching him the mechanics of football, Patrick's father taught him how to handle the game of life.

Patrick began his successful football career in high school coached by his dad, and continued on the collegiate level playing quarterback for Auburn University. As a sophomore in 1993, his team posted a perfect 11-0 record and Patrick spent the next two years as the starter and was named a team captain for his senior year.

Since graduating from Auburn in 1995, Coach Patrick Nix has coached at Jacksonville State University (AL), Henderson State University (AR), Samford University (AL), Georgia Tech (GA), and the University of Miami (FL) in such capacities as position coach, offensive coordinator, recruiting coordinator, and head coach. He has always believed coaching is a calling, and has been able to use the platform collegiate football has given him to disciple many young men. A simple Bible study with some players spawned the outline for *David Had a Dad*.

Coach Patrick Nix has been at Charleston Southern University (SC) since 2010. He lives with his wife, Krista, and their four kids, Emma Grace, Bo, Caleb, and Sara Ruth in Goose Creek, South Carolina.

You can contact the author at DavidHadaDad@hotmail.com.

Made in the USA
Charleston, SC
12 January 2012